$9 95

D1252908

OPEN GAMES

R.H.M Press

Sidney Fried, *Publisher* Lubomir Kavalek, *Editor-in-Chief*

Burt Hochberg, *Executive Editor*

Editorial Board

Anatoly Karpov, *World Champion 1975–*
Boris Spassky, *World Champion 1969–1972*
Tigran Petrosian, *World Champion 1963–1969*
Vasily Smyslov, *World Champion 1956–1957*

Contributing Editors

Svetozar Gligoric   Viktor Korchnoi
Vlastimil Hort   Bent Larsen
Borislav Ivkov   Tigran Petrosian
Anatoly Karpov   Lajos Portisch
Lubomir Kavalek   Boris Spassky

About This Book

Contrary to popular opinion, it is not difficult to play the opening reasonably well. The secret is to play reasonably.

This R.H.M. Press series, *Understanding the Chess Openings,* explains the logical basis of every move, idea, and variation in every important opening system, showing how each move plays its necessary part in the system's logical structure. The discussion, sometimes extending as far as the endgame, is presented in plain English, avoiding obscure move-analysis and imprecise symbols.

To permit this great depth and thoroughness, most openings will be treated in separate volumes. The largest systems — the Ruy Lopez and the Queen's Gambit, for example — will require two or more volumes each, and a few openings may be grouped in a single volume. If you would like to receive announcements of new volumes in this series as they are published, send your name and address to R.H.M. Press, 172 Forest Ave., Glen Cove, New York 11542.

To find out how you can stay up to date on your favorite openings, read about the *R.H.M Survey of Current Chess Openings,* described at the end of this book.

The editors thank Jeffrey Kastner, Carol Hochberg, and Richard Gardner for their invaluable assistance in the preparation of this book.

Understanding the Chess Openings

OPEN GAMES
(Except Ruy Lopez)

Edmar Mednis
International Master

Andy Soltis
International Grandmaster

William Hartston
International Master

Jack Peters
International Master

Sidney Fried, *Publisher* • Lubomir Kavalek, *Editor-in-Chief*
Burt Hochberg, *Executive Editor*

R.H.M. Press
172 Forest Avenue
Glen Cove, New York 11542

Copyright 1980
R.H.M. Press
a division of R.H.M. Associates of Delaware, Inc.
172 Forest Ave., Glen Cove., N.Y. 11542

All rights reserved. No part of this publication may be reproduced, except for brief passages in a review, stored in a
retrieval system, or transmitted, in any form or by any means, electronic, mechanical, photocopying, recording and/or
otherwise without the prior written permission of the publishers. This book may not be lent, resold, hired out or
otherwise disposed of by way of trade in any form of binding or cover other than that in which it is published, without
the prior written consent of the publishers. This book is sold subject to the Standard Conditions of Sale of Net Books
and may not be resold in the UK below the net price.

ISBN 0-89058-050-2 (R.H.M.)

Manufactured in the U.S.A.

CONTENTS

A Note on Notation

Algebraic notation is a simple grid-reference system for recording chess moves. Each square on the board is identified by a single designation (in the "descriptive" notation system each square has two names), which may be seen in the accompanying diagram.

The two forms of algebraic notation are "long" algebraic, which names the square a piece moves from and the square it moves to, and "short" or "abbreviated" algebraic, which names only the arrival square. The short form is the most common one, and it is the system used in this book. A comparison of the accompanying diagrams and the sample game score will prove the efficiency and economy of algebraic notation over the descriptive system.

It should be noted that the world chess federation (FIDE) has urged all chess publishers now using descriptive notation to convert to the algebraic system by 1981. The universal use of algebraic notation also has a practical benefit to the buyer of R.H.M. chess books: by using a single notation system, we can offer our books to a worldwide audience, thus making it possible to keep retail prices down by printing large editions.

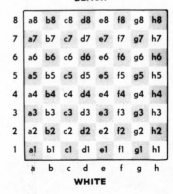

Long algebraic		Algebraic		Descriptive	
1 e2-e4	e7-e5	1 e4	e5	1 P-K4	P-K4
2 Ng1-f3	Nb8-c6	2 Nf3	Nc6	2 N-KB3	N-QB3
3 Bf1-b5	a7-a6	3 Bb5	a6	3 B-N5	P-QR3
4 Bb5-a4	Ng8-f6	4 Ba4	Nf6	4 B-R4	N-B3
5 0-0	Nf6xe4	5 0-0	Nxe4	5 0-0	NxP
6 d2-d4	b7-b5	6 d4	b5	6 P-Q4	P-QN4
7 Ba4-b3	d7-d5	7 Bb3	d5	7 B-N3	P-Q4
8 d4xe5	Bc8-e6	8 dxe5	Be6	8 PxP	B-K3
9 c2-c3	Bf8-c5	9 c3	Bc5	9 P-B3	B-QB4
10 Nb1-d2	0-0	10 Nbd2	0-0	10 QN-Q2	0-0
11 Bb3-c2	f7-f5	11 Bc2	f5	11 B-B2	P-B4
12 e5xf6	Ne4xf6	12 exf6	Nxf6	12 PxP e.p.	NxPp/3
13 Nd2-b3	Bc5-b6	13 Nb3	Bb6	13 N-N3	B-N3
14 Nf3-g5	Be6-g4	14 Ng5	Bg4	14 N-N5	B-N5
15 Bc2xh7+	Kg8-h8	15 Bxh7+	Kh8	15 BxPch	K-R1
16 Qd1-c2	Qd8-d6	16 Qc2	Qd6	16 Q-B2	Q-Q3
17 Bh7-f5	Nc6-e5	17 Bf5	Ne5	17 B-B5	N-K4
18 Nb3-d4	c7-c5	18 Nd4	c5	18 N-Q4	P-B4
19 Nd4-e6	Nf6-e4	19 Nde6	Ne4	19 N/4-K6	N-K5
20 Bf5xe4	Bg4xe6	20 Bxe4	Bxe6	20 BxN	BxN
21 Be4xd5	Be6-f5	21 Bxd5	Bf5	21 BxP	B-B4
22 Bd5-e4	Qd6-g6	22 Be4	Qg6	22 B-K4	Q-N3
23 Bc1-e3	Ra8-e8	23 Be3	Rae8	23 B-K3	QR-K1
24 Ra1-e1	Bf5xe4	24 Rae1	Bxe4	24 QR-K1	BxB
25 Qc2xe4	Ne5-f3+	25 Qxe4	Nf3+	25 QxB	N-B6ch

SYMBOLS

!	A good move.
!!	An excellent, beautiful or hard-to-find move.
?	A poor move.
??	A very poor move or a blunder.
!?	An interesting move, possibly involving some risk.
?!	A dubious move.
+	Check.

Glossary

BACKWARD PAWN: A pawn whose neighboring pawns have advanced beyond their ability to protect it. Usually a weakness, especially on an open file.

BISHOP PAIR: In general, two Bishops are stronger than two Knights or a Bishop and a Knight. This advantage is especially pronounced in uncrowded positions.

CENTER: The four central squares on the chessboard—e4, e5, d4, and d5.

CLOSED GAME: Generally, a type of position typified by crowdedness and lack of mobility. Also, an opening that begins with a move other than 1 e4.

DEVELOP: To activate a piece, usually by moving it off the first rank.

DOUBLED PAWNS: Two pawns of the same color on the same file, the result of a pawn capture. Often a weakness because the pawns cannot protect each other.

EN PASSANT: When a pawn, on its first move, advances two squares and passes an enemy pawn on an adjacent file which has already advanced to its fifth rank, the enemy pawn may capture the first pawn as though it had advanced only one square; i.e., in passing (French: *en passant*). This optional capture may be played only on the first opportunity in each instance, not later.

EN PRISE: A French phrase describing a piece or pawn on an unprotected square and subject to capture without compensation.

EXCHANGE, THE: The difference in value between a Rook and a Knight or a Bishop. Usually spelled with a capital E to avoid confusion with "exchange" in its normal meaning.

FIANCHETTO: Italian for "on the flank." The development of a Bishop on b2, g2, b7, or g7.

GAMBIT: The sacrifice of a pawn or two (sometimes a piece) in the opening to gain time or space or some other type of advantage.

HANGING PAWNS: "Hanging" is a colloquialism that means the same as EN PRISE. "Hanging pawns" is a special term to describe two adjacent pawns of the same color on their fourth rank and separated from other pawns. They are an important element in many typical middlegames, often requiring patient defense but also capable of dynamic action.

HOLE: A square in either side's camp, usually on the third rank, that can no longer be protected by a pawn. Usually a weakness in the opening and middlegame.

INITIATIVE: The momentum of a continuing series of tactical or positional threats by the same player.

GLOSSARY

ISOLATED PAWN: A pawn separated by at least one file from other pawns of the same player.

MINORITY ATTACK: A characteristic attack by a small number of pawns (the minority) against a greater number of pawns (the majority), usually with the object of reducing the majority to a weak or isolated pawn.

OPPOSITE-COLOR BISHOPS: When each side has only one Bishop and the Bishops do not travel on the same color squares, very often a certain drawish tendency enters the game, especially as the endgame approaches.

OPEN GAME: Generally, a type of position typified by clear lines, relatively few pawns, and great mobility for the pieces. Also, an opening that begins 1 e4 e5.

PASSED PAWN: A pawn that has passed all enemy pawns capable of capturing it or otherwise stopping its progress to the eighth rank. A protected passed pawn is one protected by another pawn. Connected passed pawns are two or more passed pawns on adjacent files and thus capable of protecting one another.

SACRIFICE: A voluntary offer of material for the purpose of gaining an advantage in another form, such as attack, initiative, or position.

SHARP: Precise; usually said of a move or a position which requires great accuracy in timing and calculation and is therefore associated with some risk.

TEMPO: A unit of time equivalent to one move; used to measure the relative speed at which the forces are developed, the rate at which an attack is pursued and defended against, the rapidity of a passed pawn's advance and the opponent's efforts to stop it, etc.

VARIATION: Any line of play developing from a given position.

WEAKNESS: A square, a pawn, or a part of either player's position which is vulnerable to attack or occupation by the enemy.

ZUGZWANG: German for "compulsion to move." A situation akin to "your money or your life"—any move you make is bad, but you must move.

FREE

Important
Booklet of
Recent
Open Games

We at R.H.M. Press appreciate the support you are giving our efforts to publish the finest in chess literature.

To show our appreciation, we want to send you a free booklet, containing a collection of important and instructive recent games in these openings, which we prepared after this book was printed.

To receive your copy—there is no charge or obligation—just send your name and address as follows:

U.S., Canada, Mexico, Puerto Rico:
OPEN GAMES
R.H.M. Press
172 Forest Avenue
Glen Cove, New York 11542

Europe and elsewhere:
OPEN GAMES
R.H.M. Europe
110 Strand
London WC2R OAA

Part One
The Ideas Behind the Open Games

Edmar Mednis

All openings that begin with the moves 1 e4 e5 are called open games.

In open games, piece development is rapid, there are often many unoccupied squares on the board because of pawn exchanges in the center, and Queens and Bishops can find immediate work along their "home" diagonals. A look at the above diagram shows that both sides' Queens and King's Bishops have great initial scope. If, in the interest of further rapid development, White plays an early d2-d4, Black's possible ... exd4 response will start to clear the center and create a more open position.

In open positions, Black must be

very careful not to weaken the protection of his King. For instance, if Black moves his f-pawn, White may have a devastating check with his Queen on h5. In general, Black will want to complete the development of his Kingside pieces quickly and bring his King to safety by Kingside castling. White, on his part, will also want to mobilize his forces quickly so that he will be ready to exploit any Black misstep by launching a dangerous attack against Black's King. However, because of the open nature of the positions that result from these openings, any *premature* attack will probably boomerang, and any significant weakening of *White's* King position can also turn out to be dangerous. Since the d8-h4 diagonal is open for Black's Queen, it can easily get to g5 or h4 for an attack against White's King.

In master chess, the most popular open game is the Ruy Lopez (also called the Spanish Game), which arises after 1 e4 e5 2 ♘f3 ♘c6 3 ♗b5. Although at first sight this may look like a very sharp attacking plan, it actually prepares a slow, methodical, strategical attempt to undermine Black's e5-pawn and thereby weaken his hold on the center. This unique and important opening will be covered elsewhere in this R.H.M. series.

All the other 1 e4 e5 openings are characterized by *direct and immediate action*. Most often it is White who takes this direct action, but in some cases Black selects and sets the tone.

The open games covered in this book may be divided into four categories according to their main characteristics.

A) Rapid, direct development by White

The following openings feature rapid, direct, logical development by White: Four Knights Game (Part 4), Scotch Game (Part 5), Vienna Game (Part 9), Bishop's Opening (Part 10).

In general, Black's correct approach is to follow suit by developing rapidly himself and getting his King to safety by Kingside castling. He can then look confidently ahead to the action to come in the middlegame.

The basic position in the Four Knights Game arises after **1 e4 e5 2 ♘f3 ♘c6 3 ♘c3 ♘f6.**

Both sides have rapidly developed both Knights to their best squares, aiming toward the center. White now plays **4 ♗b5,** clearing his first rank for Kingside castling while exerting some pressure against Black's e-pawn. It is true that Black

can respond symmetrically with 4 ... ♗b4 and can expect in due course to achieve approximate equality. However, the sharper **4 ... ♘d4!** is more effective. The point is, when White captures the annoying Knight by **5 ♘xd4,** Black's recapture **5 ... exd4** wins a tempo (one unit of time—see Glossary) because White's Queen Knight is attacked. White has nothing better than **6 e5,** and after **6 ... dxc3 7 exf6** both pairs of Knights have left the board. Generally, exchanging pieces early in the opening makes it easier for Black to defend because White's attacking power has been reduced. In Part 4 we will see that continued rapid development leads to further unavoidable exchanges and a solid, equal position.

The Scotch Game arises after **1 e4 e5 2 ♘f3 ♘c6 3 d4 exd4 4 ♘xd4.**

The exchange of White's d-pawn for Black's e-pawn has led to a partial clearing of the center. As a direct consequence of this, White

2

can easily complete the development of his minor pieces, and his e-pawn on the fourth rank gives him a slight superiority in the center. For Black, the exchange of central pawns means that he no longer has to worry about protecting his e-pawn, and the clearing of the center also allows him to complete the development of his Kingside smoothly. To gain full equality, Black will have to neutralize the influence of White's e-pawn by a properly timed ... d7-d5 advance. The main line of play in Part 5 illustrates these principles very well: **4 ... ♘f6 5 ♘c3 ♗b4 6 ♘xc6 bxc6 7 ♗d3 d5 8 exd5 cxd5 9 0-0 0-0.** Both sides have achieved their immediate opening objectives and are ready for interesting middlegame play with equal chances.

In the Vienna Game White gives first preference to the development of his Queen Knight: **1 e4 e5 2 ♘c3.**

By protecting his e-pawn and making the potential ... d7-d5

central advance more difficult for Black to achieve, White gains the opportunity to continue his development with minimal interference by Black. Black's most effective response is the developing move **2 ... ♘f6.** Since White is assured of at least some central influence as a result of 2 ♘c3, he can now proceed with the sharp 3 f4. However, more in the spirit of the Vienna Game is **3 ♗c4 ♘c6 4 d3 ♗b4 5 ♘f3 d6 6 0-0 ♗xc3 7 bxc3 ♘a5 8 ♗b3 ♘xb3 9 axb3 0-0,** as discussed in Part 9. Both Kings are safe, development is almost complete, and a maneuvering middlegame is in prospect.

Simple, direct development is also the theme of the Bishop's Opening: **1 e4 e5 2 ♗c4.**

White has placed his Bishop on an open, active-looking diagonal. However, since Black has not yet had to play ... ♘c6, he can proceed to challenge the Bishop with a quick ... c7-c6 and ... d7-d5. After **2 ... ♘f6 3 d3** (note that 3 ♘c3 transposes into the Vienna Game) 3

... c6 4 ♘f3 d5 5 ♗b3 ♗d6, Black is ready to castle and has at least temporarily closed the diagonal of White's King Bishop.

B) Rapid development by White with an early attack in mind

In these openings White is ready to undertake direct action as soon as he has achieved some development: Giuoco Piano (Part 2), Two Knights Defense (Part 3), Center Game/Danish Gambit (Part 10), Ponziani Opening (Part 10).

The Giuoco Piano arises after the logical developing moves 1 e4 e5 2 ♘f3 ♘c6 3 ♗c4 ♗c5.

White has developed both his King Bishop and King Knight, his Bishop is pointed at Black's potentially vulnerable f7 point, and his Knight is also available for action there. Black also wants to complete his Kingside development rapidly to minimize White's attacking prospects. For instance, after 4 0-0 ♘f6 the attack 5 ♘g5? is clearly premature, since Black

simply castles: 5 ... 0-0. The exchanging moves 6 ♗xf7 + ?! ♖xf7 7 ♘xf7 ♔xf7 leave Black with a material advantage and no positional worries.

In the diagramed position, White can choose the Evans Gambit: 4 b4, sacrificing a pawn to win an extra tempo to speed his development. Or he can aim for simple, direct development with 4 d3 followed by 5 ♘c3. However, the best way to combine development with attacking chances is 4 c3, threatening 5 d4. Since Black has no satisfactory way of preventing this, his best plan is to complete the development of his Kingside with 4 ... ♘f6!. After the indicated 5 d4 exd4 6 cxd4 Black is able to move his Bishop without loss of time by checking the White King: 6 ... ♗b4 + . Since 7 ♘c3 allows the simple 7 ... ♘xe4 (see Part 2 for the possible complications), White should play 7 ♗d2. After 7 ... ♗xd2 + 8 ♘bxd2 d5! 9 exd5 ♘xd5 10 ♕b3! ♘ce7! 11 0-0 0-0, both sides have completed their Kingside

4

development. White has the slight advantage of the more active position for the middlegame to come.

The Two Knights Defense arises when after **1 e4 e5 2 ♘f3 ♘c6 3 ♗c4** Black answers **3 ... ♘f6.**

By developing his King Knight before his King Bishop, Black applies pressure against White's e-pawn—but this leaves his f7 point vulnerable to attack. White has two logical plans now: central activity with 4 d4 or an immediate attack against Black's Kingside by **4 ♘g5.** After the essentially forced **4 ... d5 5 exd5** Black should brake White's attack by sacrificing a pawn with **5... ♘a5! 6 ♗b5 + c6! 7 dxc6 bxc6!.** After **8 ♗e2 h6** Black gains an edge in development which approximately compensates him for the sacrificed pawn. I emphasize: Black's chances for active play are much greater in the Two Knights Defense than in the Giuoco Piano—but the price is a whole pawn.

In the Danish Gambit, which is part of the Center Game, White sacrifices two pawns in five moves to speed his development: **1 e4 e5 2 d4 exd4 3 c3 dxc3 4 ♗c4 cxb2 5 ♗xb2.**

Because this is a very open position, White's edge in development can easily become decisive. Therefore, Black should not be greedy but should return one of the pawns with **5 ... d5!.** As we will see in Part 10, Black will keep the other pawn and with it a definite advantage.

Immediate activity in the center is the idea behind the Ponziani Opening, which arises after **1 e4 e5 2 ♘f3 ♘c6 3 c3.**

White plans to create a strong center with 4 d4. Since that can't be prevented, Black again does best to mobilize his kingside rapidly. **3 ... ♘f6! 4 d4 ♘xe4 5 d5 ♘e7 6 ♘xe5 ♘g6 7 ♗d3 ♘xe5 8 ♗xe4 ♗c5.** Both sides stand well and the chances are equal.

C) White attacks

White's most immediate attacking opening is the King's Gambit: **1 e4 e5 2 f4.** If Black accepts the pawn—**2 ... exf4**—the King's Gambit Accepted results.

This position is as sharp and unbalanced as a position can be. White's sacrifice of the valuable f-pawn has also seriously weakened his King position. And for what? White hopes for two things: attacking chances along the f-file and a strong center after an early d2-d4. If White can achieve both of these objectives, he will stand extremely well. Black can choose a number of specific plans. There are two basic strategies: one is to safeguard the forward f-pawn after **3 ♘f3** with 3 ... g5; the other is to try to combine defense and offense with activity in the center. The main line discussed in Part 7 uses the latter approach, starting with **3 ... d5.** In all King's Gambit positions, play becomes so sharp that it is impossible to do well without a good knowledge and understanding of the specific variations. In Part 7 the key position is reached after **4 exd5 ♘f6 5 ♗b5+ c6 6 dxc6 ♘xc6 7 d4 ♗d6 8 ♕e2+ ♗e6.** Black strives for rapid completion of his development and is ready to sacrifice a pawn after **9 ♘g5** by **9 ... 0-0!.** The middlegame will be very complicated, and the player with the greater knowledge and stouter heart will win.

D) Black chooses the opening

In a few cases, Black can select the opening and can even choose whether to set an aggressive or a defensive tone.

1) Defensive openings

The two defensive openings that Black can select are the Philidor Defense (Part 10) and the Petroff Defense (Part 6).

After 1 e4 e5 2 ♘f3, if Black defends his e-pawn not with 2 ... ♘c6 but with **2 ... d6,** the Philidor Defense arises.

Black's approach is theoretically sound, of course, yet the practical problem is that after **3 d4 ♘f6 4 ♘c3 ♘bd7 5 ♗c4! ♗e7 6 0-0 0-0** he lacks breathing room. As a consequence, in practical play White has the much easier middlegame tasks.

The Petroff Defense arises when Black responds to **1 e4 e5 2 ♘f3** with **2 ... ♘f6,** attacking White's e-pawn.

Though Black seems to be attacking, this opening is actually quite a defensive one because Black is always a move behind White and eventually will have to be content with parrying White's threats rather than developing his own. The characteristic position arises after **3 ♘xe5 d6 4 ♘f3 ♘xe4 5 d4 d5 6 ♗d3.** Although the position is highly symmetrical, the fact that White is a move ahead gives him a slight but comfortable advantage. The Petroff is inherently an equalizing or drawing defense and

is not suitable for playing to win with Black.

2) Offensive openings

If Black wants to attack at all costs, he can choose the Latvian Gambit (Part 10) or, as a response to the King's Gambit, the Falkbeer Countergambit (Part 8).

By far White's most usual second move after **1 e4 e5** is **2 ♘f3.** If Black wants to launch a vicious attack even this early, he can play **2 ... f5,** the Latvian Gambit.

In practical play, Black often does well because he is familiar with the gambit (since he has chosen to play it) whereas White is not (since he is probably not expecting it). However, Black's second move weakens his Kingside, does nothing for development, and leaves his e-pawn unprotected. White has a number of ways to exploit these factors. In the line given in Part 10, White himself becomes the attacker with **3 ♘xe5 ♕f6 4 ♘c4! fxe4 5 ♘c3 ♕g6 6 d3!.**

After **1 e4 e5 2 f4,** if accepting the King's Gambit seems too defensive to Black, or insufficiently complicated, he can challenge White with **2 ... d5,** the Falkbeer Countergambit.

Understandably enough, White must be very careful; but with the method given in Part 8 White can obtain a superior endgame and thus take the sting out of Black's plans and hopes: **3 exd5 e4 4 d3 ♘f6 5 dxe4 ♘xe4 6 ♘f3 ♗c5 7 ♕e2 ♗f5 8 ♘c3 ♕e7 9 ♗e3 ♗xe3 10 ♕xe3.**

As an overall conclusion, it can be said that Black is not theoretically justified in launching an early attack in openings that begin 1 e4 e5. However, this doesn't mean that such an approach cannot succeed in a practical game or that White can take things too easy. The point of this guide is that understanding the principles of opening play will make playing chess more fun—and will also help you score more points!

Part Two
Giuoco Piano (Italian Game)
Edmar Mednis

White	Black
1 e4	e5
2 ♘f3	♘c6
3 ♗c4	

There are two specific ideas and one general idea behind 3 ♗c4. From c4 the Bishop aims directly at f7, the most vulnerable point in the vicinity of the uncastled King. Since the Bishop also controls d5, an important central square, any plans Black may have to liberate himself with the central advance d7-d5 will be more difficult to execute. Finally, by clearing the back row of minor pieces, White is ready for Kingside castling. Early castling is usually desirable in open games because the King will generally be safer in the corner than in the

center, and the King Rook will be able to enter play quickly along either the e- or f-file.

3 ... ♗c5

This symmetrical response brings about the Giuoco Piano opening. The ideas behind Black's move are exactly the same as the ideas behind White's. Of course, since Black is half a step behind White, he should anticipate that, for the moment, he will have to do more defending than attacking.

It is fairly easy to see that c5 is the most active square for the Bishop. Sometimes Black chooses the more passive 3 ... ♗e7, which is called the Hungarian Defense. However, a direct comparison shows that White then has the more active King Bishop, and the immediate central advance **4 d4!** is good for White because he will have the more active position.

Developing the King Knight to its preferred central location first with 3 ... ♘f6 is fine too. That leads to the Two Knights Defense, which is the subject of Part Three of this volume.

4 c3!

9

After Black's third move White can choose one of three basic approaches:

1) Extreme sharpness with **4 b4,** the Evans Gambit. White sacrifices a whole pawn to gain exactly one tempo. As mentioned in Part One, a tempo is a unit of time, or, in effect, an extra move to be used to achieve a desired goal. After 4 ... ♗xb4 White continues 5 c3. By attacking the Bishop White gains one tempo for the desirable central advance 6 d4. However, Black doesn't have to return the Bishop to c5 but can position it actively by playing 5 ... ♗a5!. The Bishop is safer here than on c5, where White's 6 d4 would attack it, and more active than on e7. After 6 d4 it is very risky for Black to play the greedy 6 ... exd4?! since White's advantage in development after 7 0-0! can become very dangerous. Instead, Black should play the solid 6 ... d6! and after 7 ♕b3 defend the f-pawn with 7 ... ♕d7. If White now tries to open the position by means of 8 dxe5, it is risky for Black to recapture, but he can set up promising counterplay with 8 ... ♗b6!. Black now plans to trade his Knight for White's strong King Bishop by 9 ... ♘a5, regardless of whether White plays 9 0-0 or 9 exd6. With White's King Bishop off the board, Black will have no more worries and can expect a fully equal middlegame.

2) Quiet, sound development with **4 d3** ♘f6 5 ♘c3 d6 6 ♗g5.

This line of play best expresses the name of the opening: Giuoco Piano is Italian for "quiet game." Because Black's development has been both sound and rapid, he has nothing to fear and can break the pin with 6 ... h6!. After 7 ♗h4 the symmetrical 7 ... ♗g4 is fine for Black, and after 7 ♗xf6 ♕xf6 8 ♘d5 ♕d8 9 c3 a6 10 b4 ♗a7 Black's position is solid and sound.

3) The best of both worlds is served by **4 c3!**. White gets ready for the active central advance d2-d4 without any of the disadvantages we have seen in the other lines of play.

4 ...   ♘f6!

Since there is no satisfactory way for Black to prevent 5 d4, developing the King Knight while simultaneously attacking the e-pawn saves time and is by far the best and most logical move.

Both 4 ... ♕e7?! and 4 ... d6?! are inferior. The problem with **4 ... ♕e7** is that White plays 5 d4!

anyway! The win of a pawn by 5 ... exd4?! 6 0-0! dxc3 7 ♘xc3 is much too dangerous for Black since he is already behind in development, and White's coming 8 ♘d5 will gain more time by forcing Black's Queen to move again. The problem with **4 ... d6** is that it is too passive and White will achieve a very strong center with 5 d4 exd4 6 cxd4. Now after 6 ... ♗b4+ White can play 7 ♘c3 without the risks associated with the sacrifice of his e-pawn in the main line, or if 6 ... ♗b6 7 ♘c3 ♘f6 8 ♗e3! ♘g4 9 ♗b3! 0-0 10 ♕d3!, White has no need to fear 10 ... ♗xf3 11 gxf3 because it just serves to further strengthen White's center.

5 d4

The only logical followup to 4 c3. Of course, the solid 5 d3 is playable, but what then is the point of White's fourth move?

Often there is more than one good plan in a given opening position. Yet, once a particular plan has been chosen, one must be consistent in executing it. Skipping to and fro between various courses will lead only to indigestion!

5 ...   exd4
6 cxd4

Definitely the normal reply. A tricky move is **6 e5!?**, to try to force Black's King Knight to move, for if it actually does move he will be in trouble: 6 ... ♘g4? 7 ♗xf7+!

♔xf7 8 ♘g5+ followed by 9 ♕xg4; or if 6 ... ♘e4? then 7 ♗d5!. However, Black can exploit the position of White's King Bishop by launching a counterattack with 6 ... d5!. Whether White plays 7 exf6 dxc4 8 fxg7 ♖g8 or 7 ♗b5 ♘e4 8 cxd4 ♗b6, the complicated middlegame offers Black equal chances.

After White's actual move (6 cxd4), Black's Bishop is under attack. Retreating it—say by 6 ... ♗b6?—allows White's central pawns to move forward menacingly: 7 d5 ♘e7 8 e5 ♘g4 9 d6! and if now 9 ... ♘xf2 10 ♕b3 ♘xh1, White has the killing 11 ♗xf7+ ♔f8 12 ♗g5!. Black can, however, safeguard his Bishop with gain of time by checking White's King.

6 ...   ♗b4+

White must now decide how seriously to take Black's check. The choice is between the following three moves.

1) The risky **7 ♔f1** sets a trap based on the fact that the greedy 7

... ♘xe4? boomerangs: 8 d5! ♘e7 9 ♕d4 ♘f6 10 ♗g5 and White has a very strong attacking position. One typical example: 10 ... ♘g6 11 ♘bd2 ♗e7 12 ♖e1 0-0 13 h4! and with *all* of White's pieces ready for the attack, Black's survival chances are very slight. The correct way to exploit White's voluntary decision to give up the castling privilege is the active and thematic central advance 7 ... d5!. After 8 exd5 ♘xd5 9 ♗g5 ♕d6 10 ♘c3 ♗xc3 11 bxc3 0-0! White has no compensation for the awkward location of his King.

2) The attacking **7 ♘c3** is the move most explored by opening theory. White sacrifices his valuable e-pawn in the hope of getting enough of an attack to compensate for this loss. Black can and *should* capture this unprotected pawn. White's chances were formerly thought to be good enough to gain at least equality, but current knowledge shows that Black can successfully weather all White's thrusts. The best way of playing the variation is as follows: **7 ... ♘xe4 8 0-0** (The only sensible approach is to play for the attack.) **8 ... ♗xc3!** (Capturing with the Knight is inferior because after 8 ... ♘xc3?! 9 bxc3 gains a tempo by attacking the Bishop. To come out of the opening with only one black eye, Black must then play the developing/attacking 9 ... d5!, for the greedy 9 ... ♗xc3? is punished by 10 ♗a3!; for instance, after 10

... d5 11 ♗b5! ♗xa1 12 ♖e1+ ♗e6 13 ♕a4! ♖b8 14 ♘e5!, Black can't castle and his King is defenseless in the middle of the board. One thematic example: 14 ... ♕c8 15 ♗xc6+ bxc6 16 ♕xc6+ ♔d8 17 ♘xf7+! ♗xf7 18 ♗e7 mate!) **9 d5!?** (Again White's most active and trickiest plan. Black has nothing to fear after 9 bxc3?! d5!, followed by castling.) **9 ... ♗f6!** (After other moves White wins back the piece in a favorable way. Black's attempt to hold on to it with 9 ... ♘e5 10 bxc3 ♘xc4 11 ♕d4 ♘cd6? leads to disaster: 12 ♕xg7 ♕f6 13 ♕xf6 ♘xf6 14 ♖e1+! ♔f8 15 ♗h6+ ♔g8 16 ♖e5! ♘fe4 17 ♖ae1! f5 18 ♖e7! b6 19 ♘e5!. Black is up a piece only "on paper"—in reality he is playing without both Rooks and his Queen Bishop, whereas every one of White's pieces is participating in the attack.) **10 ♖e1 ♘e7 11 ♖xe4 d6.**

This is the critical position in the 7 ♘c3 variation. Black is a pawn ahead and, given time, will castle

Kingside and consolidate without too much difficulty. Therefore White should continue to attack. Two possibilities:

a) 12 g4 0-0! 13 g5 ♗e5 14 ♘xe5 dxe5 15 ♖xe5 ♘g6 16 ♖e1 ♕d7. White has regained the pawn but has noticeably weakened the protection of his King, which means that Black has the better chances.

b) 12 ♗g5 ♗xg5 13 ♘xg5 h6! 14 ♗b5+ (after 14 ♕h5 Black simply castles) 14 ... ♗d7 15 ♕e2 ♗xb5 16 ♕xb5+ ♕d7. If now 17 ♕e2 ♔f8!, and after the Knight retreats Black wins a second pawn with 18 ... ♘xd5. If 17 ♕xb7 instead, Black castles by 17 ... 0-0 and after 18 ♖ae1 ♘g6 19 ♘f3 ♖fb8 he will win the b-pawn and thus still have the extra pawn he won when he played 7 ... ♘xe4.

All these very complicated variations are by far the hardest lines in the Giuoco Piano to play. Because they are so complicated, not too many people actually play the 7 ♘c3 line, and therefore it is given here only as a sideline.

3) The safe, sound 7 ♗d2 is White's best move and is our main line. White reacts to the check with development and without giving up any material.

7 ♗d2 ♗xd2+

Since White's Bishop is attacking Black's, now 7 ... ♘xe4 allows the combination 8 ♗xb4 ♘xb4 9 ♗xf7+! ♔xf7 10 ♕b3+ d5 11 ♘e5+! and White recovers the piece

with some advantage because Black's King will be uncomfortable no matter where it goes.

8 ♘bxd2

Developing while protecting the e-pawn is the only correct way.

8 ... d5!

Black must challenge White's present central superiority and this is the right moment to do it.

The pseudo-sacrifice 8 ... ♘xe4 is interesting, with the idea 9 ♘xe4 d5. However, with either 10 ♗xd5 ♕xd5 11 0-0! or 10 ♕e2 0-0 11 0-0-0! White retains the greater central influence and with it a slight advantage.

9 exd5 ♘xd5
10 ♕b3!

This is by far the most active move for White, and it is also excellent from a practical standpoint because it tempts Black to go wrong in two ways:

1) **10 ... ♛e7 + ?** prevents White from castling, it is true, but after 11 ♔f1 Black must lose a piece. The attacked Knight on d5 must move, and after, say, 11 ... ♞f4 12 ♖e1! ♗e6 13 d5, the pinned Bishop is dead.

2) **10 ... ♞a5?!** forces White to part with his Bishop, but the cost—a Knight misplaced on the edge of the board—is too great: 11 ♛a4 + c6 12 ♗xd5! ♛xd5 13 0-0 0-0 14 ♖fc1!. The threat is 15 ♖c5, winning the Knight. After 14 ... b6 15 b4 ♞b7 16 ♛xc6 White has pocketed the valuable c-pawn.

10 ...   **♞ce7!**

Black's King Knight is well placed on d5 for purposes of both offense and defense, and the repositioning of the other Knight to e7—to be followed perhaps by ... c7-c6— ensures that the Knight on d5 can keep its ground.

11   0-0

Bringing the King to safety and making it possible for the King Rook to take part in the coming action.

11 ...   **0-0**

Black of course must also ensure the safety of his King.

Both sides have completed their initial developmental tasks, and it is time to evaluate the position and each side's prospects.

White will grab the e-file with his King Rook, and the pressure he exerts on the file may be increased in due course by doubling Rooks (when both Rooks stand on the same file, they are said to be doubled). He will try to use the e5 square for his King Knight and the e4 or c5 square for his Queen Knight, to apply even more pressure on Black's position.

Black will try to prevent any meaningful attacks by White and will look for opportunities to start counterplay against the one fundamental weakness in White's position: the isolated d-pawn.

At the moment, White's more active position and more advanced development give him a slight theoretical advantage. However, since there are no fundamental weaknesses in Black's position, Black may quite reasonably expect to fully neutralize White's pressure. If White becomes careless, Black will have excellent chances to get at White's isolated d-pawn.

Instructive Game No. 1

White: E. Mednis
Black: B. Spassky

World Student Team
Championship, Varna 1958

1	e4	e5
2	♘f3	♘c6
3	♗c4	♗c5
4	c3	♘f6
5	d4	exd4
6	cxd4	♗b4 +
7	♗d2	♗xd2 +
8	♘bxd2	d5
9	exd5	♘xd5
10	♕b3	♘ce7

Crazy as it seems, it may be possible to leave the attacked Knight undefended and simply castle, a suggestion by Soviet Grandmaster David Bronstein. After 10 ... 0-0!? 11 ♗xd5 ♘a5 Black gets the piece back, and although White does retain a one-pawn advantage after 12 ♗xf7 + ♖xf7 13 ♕c3 ♖e7 + 14 ♔d1, the insecure location of White's King gives Black good chances for counterplay.

11	0-0	0-0
12	♖fe1	

Taking command of the only open file is the best way for White to try to exploit his slight advantage in space.

12	...	♘b6

This attempt to make White withdraw his Bishop is double-edged, for the Knight leaves its strong position in the center. For the more solid alternative 12 ... c6, see Instructive Game No. 2.

13	♗d3	h6

Preventing any possible combinations starting with White's ♘g5. Foolhardy is 13 ... ♗e6? since the Exchange sacrifice 14 ♖xe6! is very strong: after 14 ... fxe6 White can play either 15 ♕xe6 + or 15 ♘g5, in either case with an extremely dangerous attack.

14	a4	

Since Black's Knight is already "on location" to attack this pawn, which will remain on a4, and Black's Bishop will attack it again from d7, White gains less than nothing from this advance. More promising is 14 ♖ac1!, planning 15 ♗b1 and hoping for mating threats along the b1-h7 diagonal.

14	...	a5!
15	♖ac1	♗d7
16	♕c2	♘ed5!
17	b3	♘b4
18	♕b1	♘xd3
19	♕xd3	♗e6
20	♖e5!	

White thematically tries to exploit the open e-file, and Black tries to neutralize the pressure on the file while hoping to take advantage of the vulnerability of White's pawns on b3 and d4. Overall the chances are equal.

20	...	♖e8
21	♖ce1	♘d5!
22	♕e4	♕d7
23	h3	c6
24	g4	

Increasing White's space superiority on the Kingside. White cannot afford to allow Black the time to start attacking White's weak pawns.

24	...	♖e7
25	♘h4	♖ae8
26	♕f3	♘b4!
27	♘f5	

Forcing a series of equalizing exchanges is the best White can do.

27	...	♗xf5
28	♖xe7	♖xe7
29	♖xe7	♕xe7
30	♕xf5	

The Queen-and-Knight endgame offers equal chances, and the simplest way to maintain the equality is the solid 30 ... ♘d5. Instead, Spassky decides to create some complications.

| 30 | ... | g6!? |
| 31 | ♕xa5! | |

Why not?

31	...	♘d3
32	♘f1	♘f4
33	♕e5!	♘xh3+
34	♔g2	♕xe5
35	dxe5	♘f4+
36	♔g3	♘d3
37	f4	g5?!

By playing to win an ultimately unimportant pawn on the Kingside, Black risks losing the game on the Queenside. The position calls for 37 ... ♘c5 38 ♘d2 ♔f8! followed by 39 ... ♔e7, and Black should draw without much difficulty.

38	fxg5	hxg5
39	♘d2!	♘xe5?!
40	♘e4!	♘d7
41	a5!	

The game was adjourned here, and White sealed his 41st move. The endgame is far superior for White because he wins Black's b-pawn. A full night of perfect analysis by the Soviet team, however, allowed Black to draw by exactly one hair.

41	...	♔f8!
42	♘d6	♘c5!
43	♘xb7!	♘a6!

Blockading the a-pawn is an absolute requirement. Of course, both 43 ... ♘xb7?? and 43 ... ♘xb3?? allow the a-pawn a decisive run after 44 a6.

44	♔f3	♔e7
45	♔e4	c5!!
46	♔d5	f5!!

The advanced g-pawn gives Black just enough counterplay to draw.

47	♘xc5!	fxg4
48	♘e4	♔d8!
49	♔c6	g3
50	♘xg3	♔c8
51	♘e4	g4
52	♔b6	♘b4
53	♔b5	♘c2
54	♔c5?!	

This allows Black to set up a blockade which draws easily. Black's task would be considerably harder after 54 b4!, although 54 ... ♔b7 55 ♔a4 ♘d4 does just hold.

54	...	♔b7
55	b4	♔a6!
56	♘g3	♘a3
57	♘e2	♘c2
	Draw	

Instructive Game No. 2

White: J. Mestel
Black: V. Hort

Hastings 1977/78

1	e4	e5
2	♘f3	♘c6
3	♗c4	♗c5
4	c3	♘f6
5	d4	exd4
6	cxd4	♗b4+
7	♗d2	♗xd2+
8	♘bxd2	d5
9	exd5	♘xd5
10	♕b3	♘ce7
11	0-0	0-0
12	♖fe1	c6

The solid alternative to the double-edged 12 ... ♘b6. Black ensures that the Knight on d5 will have sufficient support and makes c7 and b6 accessible to his Queen.

13 a4!

This time the advance of the a-pawn is an absolutely correct attempt to gain Queenside space because this time the pawn will not be vulnerable since Black has played ... c7-c6, closing the d7-a4 diagonal.

13 ... a5!

Further encroachment by White's a-pawn should be prevented. Inferior moves are: (a) 13 ... ♛b6?! 14 a5! and the endgame after the exchange of Queens is better for White because he has more space all over the board; (b) 13 ... ♘g6?! 14 ♗xd5! and it will be uncomfortable for Black to defend his isolated d-pawn.

14 ♘e4 ♛b6!

It is safest for Black to offer the exchange of Queens. Developing the Bishop by 14 ... ♗f5 allows White to keep up the pressure with 15 ♘g3 ♗g6 16 ♘e5.

15	♘c3	♛xb3
16	♗xb3	h6

Preventing the possibility of mate on his first rank, and also planning 17 ... ♗e6 without being bothered by White's ♘g5. White therefore decides on a double exchange on d5, forcing Black to accept an isolated d-pawn.

17	♘xd5	♘xd5
18	♗xd5	cxd5
19	♖e7!	

With an active Rook on the 7th rank, White seems to have achieved the better endgame. However ...

19	...	♖a6!!
	Draw	

Black's Rook will find a great location on b6, where it will attack White's b-pawn and at the same time protect Black's own b-pawn. This will then allow Black's Bishop to be developed, which will lead to fully equal chances.

The agreement to call it a draw seems a little premature, but it is theoretically well justified. Both players realize that the chances are equal and trust each other's skill.

Part Three
Two Knights Defense

Andy Soltis

Among the openings that begin 1 e4 e5 the Two Knights has relatively simple strategical ideas. Its tactical situations, however, make it one of the most complex to play—for White and Black. It is aggressive and violent, and often the momentum shifts dramatically from one player to the other in the space of a single move. Evaluating the positions reached after eight or ten moves is difficult because often one side has a material advantage while, across the board, the other side has the greater piece activity. In the main line it is Black who sacrifices a pawn, but in some other lines it is White who gives up material to create attacking chances.

The Two Knights *Defense* may be a misnomer, because the opening is actually a counterattack. (In fact, the Soviets sometimes call it the "Tchigorin Counterattack," after the great 19th century Russian master.) Black's philosophy is quite different here than in the Giuoco Piano.

White	Black
1 e4	e5
2 ♘f3	♘c6
3 ♗c4	♘f6!?

Black decides to anticipate the attack on f7 with threatening moves of his own. Before White can augment the assault on f7 with more pieces (by means of ♘g5, or c2-c3 and ♕b3), Black hopes to be castled into safety. If castling is denied him because of a crisis in the center, he will blunt the attack on f7 with ... d7-d5, or ... ♘xe4 followed by ... d7-d5. If White decides not to attack f7 immediately, White will be forced to defend his e-pawn, after which Black can achieve a secure defensive position with Knights on c6 and f6, and Bishops on c5 (or e7) and g4 (or e6).

4 ♘g5

Siegbert Tarrasch, a world championship challenger and one of the very greatest players in chess history, called this a poor, beginner's move. Yet it is the logical next step in White's strategy of attacking f7, and today, nearly a century since Tarrasch's heyday, it is considered White's best bet for an advantage. Black is forced to meet the threats to f7 by opening the position or mounting his own attack on White's King.

As we'll see, in the main line that flows from 4 ♘g5 Black obtains a lead in development and good open lines for his pieces in exchange for a pawn. But many players prefer not to be cast in the role of defender when playing White—even if the position is theoretically in White's favor—and would rather make the threats than answer them. For those players, **4 d4** is the alternative.

Then it is White, not Black, who is opening the center and it is White who profits after, say, **4 ... ♘xd4?** 5 ♗xf7+! ♔xf7 6 ♘xe5+ ♔g8 7 ♕xd4; or 4 ... d6 5 ♘g5 (with an improved version of the 4 ♘g5 variation because White has already played d2-d4! to aid his attack). Black gets an inferior position in the center also after **4 ... ♘xe4** 5 dxe5 ♗c5 6 0-0 because his pieces are not securely anchored there, and he must do something about the threat of 7 ♕d5, which would win material.

After 4 d4 Black should play **4 ... exd4** and place the responsibility for having opened the position on White's shoulders. White cannot quietly recapture on d4 because Black grabs the e-pawn, as planned on his third move. The counterattacking nature of the opening is clear after 4 ... exd4 5 ♘xd4? ♘xe4! 6 ♗xf7+ ♔xf7! 7 ♕h5+ g6 8 ♕d5+ ♔g7 (safe) 9 ♘xc6 bxc6 10 ♕xe4 and now 10 ... ♕e8! 11 ♕xe8 ♗b4+ followed by 12 ... ♖xe8. Black has secured his King and is forcing matters with his better developed pieces. The same is true also after 6 ♕e2 ♘xd4 7 ♕xe4+ ♕e7 or 6 ♕h5 ♘d6.

After 4 ... exd4 White has two moves which are consistent with his play. He can castle—making ... ♘xe4 risky for Black because of the open e-file—or he can press onward in the center with 5 e5. Castling is the riskier of the two, even for White, because Black will either be able to protect and keep his extra pawn at d4 or grab a second pawn, as we'll see a little later. The second idea, **5 e5**, leads to this:

Position after 4 d4 exd4 5 e5

Black must now make an important decision about his center. If he plays **5 ... ♘e4,** White can continue 6 ♗d5 or 6 ♕e2 (followed by 0-0 and ♖d1), forcing Black's Knight back to c5 and from there to e6. Black will sooner or later have to push his d-pawn one or two squares, and White will anticipate that advance by bringing his pieces to bear on d5 and d6, for instance by occupying d5 or using a Rook to control the d-file. Black may achieve equality in a theoretical sense, but his position can be somewhat constricted and difficult to play while White's pieces are bearing down on the d-file.

The other Knight move that isn't really a retreat is **5 ... ♘g4.** Again White can protect his e-pawn and anticipate changes in the center with 6 ♕e2!. This move threatens h2-h3 to kick the Knight back to h6, where its capture by White's Bishop would badly disrupt Black's Kingside pawns. Black should meet 6 ♕e2 with 6 ... ♕e7, but after 7 ♗f4 d6 White's pieces will profit somewhat from the opening of the center after 8 exd6 ♕xe2+ 9 ♗xe2 ♗xd6 10 ♗xd6 cxd6 11 ♘a3 followed by ♘b5xd4 or ♘c4.

Therefore the Knight on f6 should not be moved. The move that is most consistent with the theme of Black's counterattacking opening and that also avoids the problems that result from advancing the d-pawn later is the immediate **5 ... d5.** White should then avoid 6 exf6 dxc4 because he will have little compensation for the pawn and for Black's edge of Bishop vs. Knight. After 7 fxg7 ♗xg7 8 0-0 0-0 White doesn't even have an advantage in development, and Black's King is perfectly safe.

So White justifies his 5 e5 with **6 ♗b5!,** pinning Black's Queen Knight, and he will reinforce the pin with ♘xd4. The advantage of this policy is that White can damage Black's Queenside pawns and maintain a powerfully centralized Knight at d4 after 6 ... ♘e4 7 ♘xd4 ♗d7 8 ♗xc6! bxc6 9 0-0. Black again enjoys the theoretical benefit of having a long-range Bishop in exchange for a short-range Knight, but in this case the Knight is so well placed and Black's Bishop so restricted that White stands very well. He can continue with f2-f3, to kick out the Black Knight, and follow with f3-f4-f5 and perhaps -f6! to weaken Black's Kingside. Black can mobilize his own pawns with ... c6-c5, or he can anticipate White's pawn advance with ... f7-f6, which would enable him to fight for the opened lines on the Kingside if White's e-pawn is exchanged for Black's f-pawn.

An important finesse for White in his efforts to improve on this line is **5 0-0** (instead of 5 e5) and after **5 ... ♗c5,** then **6 e5.**

After 4 d4 exd4 5 0-0 ♗c5 6 e5

Now **6 ... d5** permits White to play **7 exf6 dxc4** and a subsequent fxg7 at a time when Black cannot recapture immediately on g7 because he has already moved his Bishop. (It is even worse for Black if he plays 5 ... ♗e7 instead of 5 ... ♗c5, because then White continues 6 e5! d5? 7 exf6 dxc4 8 fxe7!, winning a piece.)

But this difference between 5 0-0 and 5 e5 is not enough to turn the game clearly in White's favor. True, in answer to **8 fxg7** Black has to play 8 ... ♖g8. But Black will then continue with ... ♗e6, move his Queen, and castle on the Queenside. Eventually he will be able to capture the pawn at g7 and make good use of the ready-made attacking line directed against White's King at g1.

This variation, named for the 19th century German master Max Lange, is one of the hardest to evaluate. After a typical line—9 ♗g5 ♗e7 10 ♗xe7 ♔xe7! (to retain control of d4) 11 ♖e1 + ♗e6—Black's King is relatively safe (and will be safer still after it goes to f8) and he will enjoy a material advantage after ... ♖xg7.

White can push the game into complex attacks and counterattacks with **8 ♖e1 +** (instead of 8 fxg7) ♗e6 10 ♘g5! setting the trap 9 ... ♕d7? 10 ♘xe6 fxe6 11 ♕h5 + and 12 ♕xc5 with an extra piece. Black should play 9 ... ♕d5! and then try to weather the storm after 10 ♘c3! ♕f5 11 ♘ce4 0-0-0!.

This critical position has many pluses and minuses for each player. Black's Kingside will be in ruins after fxg7 and ♘xe6, but he will have a powerful set of center pawns that can support ... d4-d3-d2!, a thrust that may push White's pieces off the board. White can harass Black's Queen with g2-g4, but he will face great danger if the g-file is ever opened. Black also has a lead in development, and this will count heavily if White tries to simplify, say with 12 fxg7 ♖hg8 13 ♘xc5? ♕xc5 14 ♖xe6!? fxe6 15 ♘xe6 ♕d5 16 ♘xd8 ♖xg7! threatening mate. The chances appear to be equal after 6 e5.

Moreover, Black has alternatives along the way. The most pugnacious is to meet 5 0-0 with **5 ... ♘xe4.**

After 4 d4 exd4 5 0-0 ♘xe4

Here White doesn't even get to disrupt Black's pieces with e4-e5. He must instead try to exploit the open file with **6 ♖e1**. But there follows **6 ... d5!**. Now, since White is two pawns behind, he is committed to the attack. Through the miracle of chess tactics he can regain one of those pawns with a gain of time by playing **7 ♗xd5! ♛xd5 8 ♘c3**. Even though the Knight appears to be capturable in two different ways, one of those ways is illegal (8 ... ♘xc3) and the other simply too horrible (8 ... dxc3?? 9 ♛xd5), so Black must move his Queen. But he will stand well once he can castle, and this usually means castling Queenside. For example, **8 ... ♛a5 9 ♖xe4 + ♗e6 10 ♘xd4 0-0-0!** is fine for Black who is better developed and has a powerful pin along the d-file. White should play the subtle **9 ♘xe4,** postponing the recapture on d4 and threatening a murderous discovered check (♘f6 + , etc.). But even then Black has adequate chances with 9 ... ♗e6 10 ♘eg5 0-0-0! 11 ♘xe6 fxe6 12 ♖xe6 ♗d6. Black's pieces are all well placed and he can keep the d-pawn (13 ♘xd4?? ♘xd4 14 ♛xd4 ♗xh2 + and 15 ... ♖xd4).

These lines differ somewhat from many encountered in 1 e4 e5 openings in that here the strengths and liabilities of both sides are clearly defined. The positions arising after 4 d4 are less likely to result in a draw than the type of middlegame you find after ten moves of the Scotch Game or the Four Knights Game. It is very valuable for an inexperienced player to try the White and Black sides of these sharp openings so that he can feel comfortable with typical positions.

Anyway, back to 4 ♘g5.

Some early players more than a century ago suggested that 1 ... e5 was a mistake (!) because it led to positions like this, in which f7 is exposed to immediate attack. After 1 ... e6, the French Defense, for example, Black never has to worry about the combined attacks of Bishop and Knight directed at that poorly protected square so close to his King.

4 ...   d5

Believe it or not, Black can ignore the attacks on f7 and survive. To do so he must have violent threats of his own, to draw White's attention away from f7 and its environs and get him to worry about his own side of the board. The only way to create such violent counterthreats is **4 ... &c5**, which is known in Europe as the Traxler Counterattack, after a Czech analyst, and elsewhere as the Wilkes-Barre Variation, after the Pennsylvania chess club at which it was studied and refined.

After 4 ... &c5 Black will meet **5 &xf7**—which forks his Queen and Rook—with **5 ... &xf2 + !**. If White takes the Bishop, Black will be able to get his pieces into action with checks and threats; e.g., 6 &xf2 &xe4 + 7 &e3 &h4! 8 &xh8 &f4 +, or 7 &g1 &h4 8 &f3 &d4. Even after White's better 7 &g1 &h4 8 g3 &xg3! 9 &xh8! &d4, the strength of Black's attack forces White to accept a perpetual series of checks after 10 hxg3 &xg3 + 11 &f1 &f4 + 12 &g2 &g5 +. There is a similar story to the subtle 6 &f1 (instead of 6 &xf2) &e7 7 &xh8 because even with a little more time for defense White is under heavy assault after 7 ... d5! 8 exd5 &d4 (threatening 9 ... &g4).

White's best attempt to refute the Wilkes-Barre Variation is **5 &xf7 +**, rather than the greedy 5 &xf7. Black will move his King to e7 so that he can attack along the f-file after ... &f8. But White can return the extra pawn at the right moment to take advantage of Black's vulnerable King. For instance, 5 ... &e7 6 &d5 &f8 7 &f3 d6 8 c3 &g4 9 &xc6 and 10 d4!. Then it is White's attack, not Black's attack or White's advantage in material, that will shape the course of the middlegame.

5 exd5

No other move makes any sense. White wants to clear d5 and all the squares that lead from c4 to f7.

5 ...   &a5

This move makes a poor first impression. How can it be good for Black to put his Knight at the edge of the board? As you follow the main line you'll see that the Knight doesn't get back into action for at least half a dozen moves. There surely must be something better, you may think, such as the logical 5 ... &xd5.

And there are two answers to these basic questions. One is that 5 ... &a5 solves the crucial strategic problem of Black's opening: how to deal with the attack on f7. No other fifth move can do that; no other move immediately forces the White Bishop off the b3-f7 diagonal.

The second answer is more involved. The Knight move is best because the other moves are worse. And this needs a closer look.

1) 5 ... &xd5.

After 5 ... &xd5

It's no surprise that this is the oldest move in this position, the one Italian merchants chose when the modern rules of chess caught on some five centuries ago. Those early players quickly found a reason to doubt 5 ... ♘xd5—the reason was **6 ♘xf7!?**—and they found a name for the variation **6 ... ♔xf7 7 ♕f3+.** They called it the "Fegatello" or "Fried Liver" Attack because, in an idiom popular at the time, whether Black plays 7 ... ♔e8 8 ♗xd5 or tries to hold on to his extra material with 7 ... ♔e6, he will be as dead as a piece of fried liver.

Black's defenses have been strengthened since the 15th century, but White still enjoys a tremendous attack after 7 ... ♔e6 8 ♘c3 ♘b4! 9 ♕e4! c6 10 a3 ♘a6 11 d4 ♘c7 12 ♗f4! ♔f7 13 ♗xe5 and has sacrificed relatively little material for it (White has two pawns in exchange for a Knight). If this is not convincing, White can play 6 d4 instead of 6 ♘xf7. For example, 6 ... exd4 7 0-0 ♗e7? 8 ♘xf7! with an improved "Fegatello" because d2-d4 and 0-0 are more useful to White than ... exd4 and ... ♗e7 are to Black in comparison with the 6th-move ♘xf7 sacrifice.

2) 5 ... ♘d4 is another alternative to 5 ... ♘a5 that seems to make more sense. Black's Knight certainly covers more important squares (f3, e2, c2, f5) on d4 than it does on a5. But there is a drawback to 5 ... ♘d4: Black's Knight is not secure on that outpost square since White can

safely play c2-c3. Here he can do it immediately with **6 c3!**, which gives Black the problem of finding a new haven for the Knight. It would be secure on f5, but White has gained enough time with c2-c3 so that after 6 ... ♘f5 he can play 7 d4 exd4 8 0-0!. White's development will be almost complete after 8 ... dxc3 9 ♘xc3, while Black's will be far behind.

The critical test of 5 ... ♘d4 6 c3 is **6 ... b5.** An exchange of pieces would help Black (e.g., 7 cxd4 bxc4 8 dxe5 ♕xd5!) and it seems that White's Bishop has no good square to retreat to. But **7 ♗f1!** is the star move which forces Black to come to a decision about his Knight. He cannot retreat it without surrendering the b-pawn, so he must enter the complications that follow **7 ... ♘xd5,** which threatens 8 ... ♕xg5. White has active ways of meeting this latest Black counterattacking move, but the best reply is another "quiet" move, **8 ♘e4!.** Then Black's compensation for the pawn he must lose is dubious. For example, 8 ... ♘e6 9 ♗xb5+ ♗d7 10 ♗xd7+ ♕xd7 11 0-0 and 12 d4, or 8 ... ♕h4 9 ♘g3 ♗g4 (another counterattack) 10 f3 e4!? 11 cxd4 ♗d6 12 ♗xb5+ and 13 0-0.

The message of such a line is clear. Eventually Black may run out of counterthreats and then will have to pay for his unsound play.

3) 5 ... ♗g4 is yet another counterattacking idea, this one based on 6 f3 ♘a5! 7 ♗b5+ ♗d7. White's extra f2-f3 move, compared with the similar line after 5 ... ♘a5, is only a weakening that improves Black's chances, especially if he can put his King Bishop on c5 and prevent White from castling.

This time, however, White can meet a Black counterthreat with a counter-counterthreat: **6 ♘xf7!**, a surprise offer to exchange Queens indirectly. Black must turn down the offer because 6 ... ♗xd1 7 ♘xd8 leaves him two pawns down and with two pieces exposed to capture. He must also avoid 6 ... ♔xf7 because of 7 dxc6 discovered check. Instead, Black is better served by 6 ... ♕e7, preserving his own Queen and threatening White's Knight and Queen. But White can insert 7 d6!, which protects his Knight by opening the diagonal of his Bishop and does so with a gain of time by again attacking Black's Queen. Then 7 ... cxd6 8 f3 ends the tactical duel in White's favor because all of White's pieces are protected while Black's Bishop and King Rook are under attack.

4) 5 ... b5. This final counterattacking alternative is an attempt to improve on 5 ... ♘d4.

If White retreats the Bishop to b3, Black plays his Knight to d4 and will capture the Bishop when the need arises. (Black never gets a chance to take that Bishop in the line 5 ... ♘d4 6 c3 b5 7 ♗f1!.)

White should not be startled by moves like 5 ... b5. It is tempting to exchange off pieces with 6 dxc6 bxc4

but Black's chances of grabbing White's pawn at c6 are just as good as White's chances to grab its rival at c4 (7 ♕e2 ♕d5). White should resist exchanging his Bishop for a Black Knight in such an open position, for open positions favor the long-range pieces.

Also, 6 ♗xb5 is not accurate because 6 ... ♕xd5! simultaneously attacks White's Bishop and g-pawn. To maintain his extra pawn White would either have to give up his Bishop (7 ♗xc6 + ♕xc6) or retreat it to f1. While something can be said for these moves, consider how clever **6 ♗f1!** is. If Black recaptures on d5 with his Queen, White will play 7 ♘c3!, attacking the Queen and winning time to play 8 ♗xb5 or 8 ♘xb5. If Black decides not to take the pawn on d5 and plays 6 ... ♘d4, then after 7 c3 he will have transposed into the inferior position we examined above: 5 ... ♘d4 6 c3 b5 7 ♗f1!.

Of course, Black can recapture on d5 with his Knight rather than his Queen. But after **6 ... ♘xd5** White plays **7 ♗xb5!** and we appreciate the cleverness of 6 ♗f1. White has managed to lose a move (by playing ♗c4-f1-b5 instead of ♗b5 directly). But he has also managed to avoid the powerful centralization of Black's Queen on d5, with its double attack on Bishop (b5) and pawn (g2). Thus, after 5 ... b5 6 ♗f1! ♘xd5 7 ♗xb5 Black must play something like 7 ... ♗b7 8 d4 exd4 9 0-0 ♗e7 when it is apparent that White has the more dangerous threats after 10 ♕h5!.

We've seen that Black has several ways of continuing without putting his Knight out of play at a5. Nevertheless, it is that strange Knight move which best restricts White's pieces. Black may have to sacrifice a pawn, as we will see, but he obtains much more counterplay than in the lines just considered because the center is swept open before White can castle.

After 5 ... ♘a5

6   ♗b5 +

In the last century it was popular

for White to hold on to his extra pawn and simultaneously keep the center closed with **6 d3**. Black can meet that move with 6 ... ♘xd5, re-establishing material equality, but 7 ♕f3 ! is embarrassing; Black has to answer the latest attack on f7 with 7 ... ♗e6, which is bad (8 ♘xe6 followed by ♕h5 + and ♕xe5), or with 7 ... ♘f6, which is worse (8 ♘xf7).

Black should reconcile himself to remaining a pawn down after 6 d3 and should play **6 ... h6! 7 ♘f3 e4!**, harassing White's Knight. This is an important theme in the Two Knights Defense, since the White Knight will have a difficult time finding a haven once Black starts making threats of his own. It doesn't have much of a future on d4 (8 ♘d4 ♗c5) and, since 8 dxe4 leaves White's Bishop unprotected on c4, his best try is to confuse the issue with **8 ♕e2!**.

This move prevents 8 ... exf3 and, by protecting the Bishop, threatens 9 dxe4. Black must leave the center relatively closed with **8 ... ♘xc4 9 dxc4 ♗c5** and castle as quickly as he can. Since White must spend a move on retreating his Knight, Black will have a substantial lead in development.

The position after 9 ... ♗c5 is considered to be dangerous for White because Black will be able to open the position for his superior minor pieces with ... b7-b5 or ... c7-c6 or even ... e4-e3! once he has castled. If White doesn't play h2-h3 soon, Black will also have ... ♗g4!, attacking the White Queen. The Black pawn at e4 plays a powerful role in driving the White Knight away from f3 and in making f2-f3 an extremely risky move for White to play.

The strength of Black's position is shown by two sample lines. One begins with **10 ♘fd2** 0-0 11 ♘b3 ♗g4!, after which White has no good place for his Queen; he is clearly worse after 12 ♕f1 ♗b4+! 13 c3 ♗e7 followed by ... ♘d7-e5-d3!. The second line is **10 h3** (stopping ... ♗g4 and providing another retreat for the Knight) 10 ... 0-0 11 ♘h2 c6! 12 dxc6 e3! 13 ♗xe3 ♗xe3 14 fxe3 (13 ♕xe3?? ♖e8) ♘e4!, threatening 15 ... ♘g3 or 15 ... ♕h4+, and also threatening to take over the open e-file and, after ... bxc6, the half-open b-file.

But the best argument in favor of 6 ♗b5+ rather than 6 d3 is that the check is not easy to meet.

6 ...   c6

The problem with **6 ... ♗d7** is 7 **♕e2!**. Then Black is in danger of losing a second pawn; e.g., 7 ... ♗xb5 8 ♕xb5+ c6 (to protect the Knight at a5) 9 dxc6 bxc6 10 ♕xe5+ or 9 ... ♘xc6 10 ♕xb7!. Black can try to extract some compensation from the position after 7 ♕e2 by playing 7 ... ♗d6 and then 8 ♘c3 0-0. But without any clear attacking lines for his pieces and with only a slight lead in development—Black's Knight at a5 might just as well be undeveloped back at b8—he has little claim to equality.

If Black wants to play 6 ... ♗d7 he can find reasonable play for his pieces with 7 ♕e2 ♗e7 8 ♘c3 0-0, hoping that White will play 9 ♕xe5 and give Black the open e-file after 9 ... ♗d6 and 10 ... ♖e8+. With 7 ... ♗e7 Black keeps an attack on the pawn at d5 (which he doesn't have after 7 ... ♗d6 because that move blocks the d-file) and can play ... c7-c6 later. This leads to positions superficially similar to but rather different from the main line (6 ... c6): White is a bit better developed here because Black has spent time on 6 ... ♗d7, but after ... c7-c6 Black will be able to bring his Knight on a5 back into the game by recapturing on c6 with it after dxc6.

As we said, there is a problem with 6 ... ♗d7 7 ♕e2!, but it is a playable alternative for Black. With 6 ... c6 Black refuses to give White even a one-move respite.

7 dxc6   bxc6

Recapturing with the Knight would allow White to develop easily once again, but worse, it would invite him to resume that old plan, the attack on f7 (7 ... ♞xc6 8 ♗c4!).

8 ♗e2

The Bishop would not only be misplaced on a4, it would even be hanging if Black continued with his counterattack (8 ♗a4 h6! 9 ♞f3 e4! 10 ♞e5 ♛d4!—attacking two pieces—11 ♗xc6+ ♞xc6 12 ♞xc6 ♛c5 and wins the piece).

White might try to anticipate Black's plan of ... h7-h6 and ... e5-e4 with **8 ♗d3?!**, an even stranger retreat. Despite the move's obvious drawback of locking in White's d-pawn (and, as a result, his Queenside pieces), it permits him to retreat his Knight to the active e4 square. But after 8 ♗d3 Black has no need for ... h7-h6, since he can attack White's advanced Knight with 8 ... ♞d5, and with White's King Bishop on d3, White can't defend g5 with d2-d3. Black will have more than a pawn's worth of piece activity once he gets his Knight to f4; e.g., 8 ♗d3 ♞d5 9 ♞e4 f5 10 ♞g3 ♞f4!, and since White must either permit ... ♞xg2+ or lose more time with ♗f1, he clearly isn't doing as well as he does in the main line (8 ♗e2).

But there is one other way for White to meet the threat of ... cxb5 and also anticipate ... h7-h6. This is **8 ♛f3**, which pins Black's c-pawn (8 ... cxb5 9 ♛xa8) and also covers the e4 square for a possible Knight retreat. If Black takes the time to defend c6 he may lose the momentum of his attack—what chess players call the "initiative." For example, 8 ... ♛c7 9 ♗d3 h6 10 ♞e4 ♞d5 11 0-0 ♞f4 12 ♞g3 and we can see that White is already castled and ready to take over the attack with ♖e1 (threatening ♛xf4) or ♗f5 and d2-d3. Black can try to retain his initiative with further sacrifices; for instance, 8 ... cxb5 9 ♛xa8 ♛d7 followed by ... ♗c5, ... 0-0 and ... ♗b7. But a much simpler sacrifice is 8 ... ♖b8 so that on 9 ♗xc6+ ♞xc6 10 ♛xc6+ ♞d7 Black has threats of ... ♛xg5 and ... ♗b7. Although Black is now two pawns behind, his attack is too violent to ignore after, say, 11 d3 ♗e7 12 ♞f3 0-0 followed by ... ♗b7 (or, after 13 ♛e4, by 13 ... ♖b4! 14 ♛e2 e4! 15 dxe4 ♞c5 16 ♞c3 ♗a6).

Black's Queen Bishop and Queen Rook are added to his attack so quickly in these lines that perhaps White should avoid taking the pawn on c6. But even after 8 ♛f3 ♖b8 and now 9 ♗e2 ♗c5 10 0-0 0-0 and ... ♗g4, or 9 ♗d3 h6 10 ♞e4 ♞d5 11 ♞g3 g6! followed by ... ♗g7 and ... f7-f5, Black has good chances. His Rook plays an inhibiting role along the b-file and White will have serious problems completing his development.

8	...		h6
9	♞f3		

30

Two world champions, Bobby Fischer in this century and Wilhelm Steinitz in the last, tried to show that 9 ♘h3 is a good move in this position, perhaps the best move. The idea behind the strange retreat is clear: Black doesn't get to attack White's Knight again with ... e5-e4. White may even benefit from the Knight's position on h3 by being able to play f2-f4 after castling and moving his King to h1.

But 9 ♘h3 has never been popular, probably because it appears to completely disregard King safety by permitting ... ♗xh3. Then Black may regain the pawn he has sacrificed by eventually capturing the weakling on h3. Fischer showed, however, that this takes a lot of time and sharply reduces Black's advantage in time and development. Trading away his good Bishop also cuts Black's attacking chances, since it will not be very easy for him to attack White's weaknesses at h3 and g2 without it. Black's best procedure appears to be 9 ... ♗c5 10 0-0 0-0 11 d3 ♘d5, delaying ... ♗xh3 until he can get some immediate benefit from the capture. White may be able to avert ... ♗xh3, but only by playing ♔h1 and ♘g1; in the meantime, Black will coordinate his Queenside pieces with ... ♘b7, ... ♗b6, and ... ♘c5.

The position is difficult to evaluate, but it's quite playable for White. Before adopting 9 ♘h3 as part of your opening repertoire, you should familiarize yourself with your

defensive chances after ... ♗xh3 and gxh3. In most cases ♔h1 is enough to secure the King's position, but sometimes ♗f3-g2 is needed.

Position after 9 ♘f3

9	...	e4

Black must hit quickly or White will play d2-d3 and develop a solid position in the center with his pieces undisturbed. Remember that Black's Knight is still stranded out there on a5 and it will take some time to get it back into action. For now, Black must be prepared to attack without it.

10	♘e5

And there is no real choice here. If White had to retreat to g1, Black would have too great a lead in development after ... ♗c5 and ... ♕d4 or ... ♕b6.

10	...	♗d6

31

The Knight seems highly vulnerable on e5, and Black prepares to exploit it. The Bishop move anticipates d2-d4 or f2-f4, and by capturing en passant Black will give his Bishop and other pieces more room.

It seems a pity that Black can't get more out of the position than that. But if Black tries the more aggressive **10 ... ♛d4** White has surprising resources. That move does prevent d2-d4, and it also threatens the Knight; perhaps more important, it prepares ... ♝c5. However, 11 f4 is more than adequate for White. If Black captures the pawn en passant as planned (11 ... exf3), White gains time by recapturing with his Knight and simultaneously attacking Black's Queen. If Black leaves the pawn alone and plays the dangerous-looking 11 ... ♝c5, he will find that White is not only safe after 12 ♖f1 but also threatens to win a piece with 13 c3 and 14 b4. After White gets those pawn moves played, he will either win material or be able to defend his position comfortably.

There is more logic behind **10 ... ♛c7**; now on 11 f4 Black can play either 11 ... ♝c5 or 11 ... exf3 en passant (with the important difference that now 12 ♞xf3 will not attack Black's Queen). The en passant capture should lead into the same lines as 10 ... ♝d6 11 f4 exf3 12 ♞xf3 (discussed below). And 11 ... ♝c5 again invites 12 c3 followed by b2-b4. For example, 11 ... ♝c5 12 c3 ♞b7 13 b4 ♝b6 (to keep White from

castling) 14 a4 a6 15 ♞a3 followed by ♞c4 and either ♞xb6 or (if Black retreats the Bishop to a7) ♞e3. Then White can castle, play ♔h1, and eventually disentangle his pieces with d2-d4!.

Position after 10 ... ♝d6

With Black's Bishop on d6 rather than c5, White's problems multiply. Assuming the likelihood that Black will capture en passant whether White plays f2-f4 or d2-d4, we must consider what the next half dozen moves will look like. After **11 d4** exd3 12 ♞xd3 Black strengthens the attack on the b8-h2 diagonal with 12 ... ♛c7 and follows this with ... c6-c5-c4 or ... ♞d5 or just ... ♝a6 and ... ♖d8. On the other hand, if White plays **11 f4** exf3 12 ♞xf3 he has a weaker Kingside and a problem in developing his Queenside pieces. (Finally, we should mention that White can also meet the threat to his Knight by simply moving it. But whether it goes to g4 or c4—the Knight's fifth move so far—White has only postponed the question of which center pawn he will advance. For more on this see the first illustrative game.)

The choice between 11 f4 and 11 d4 has been The Great Debate of the Two Knights Defense for several years. The d-pawn is the more natural one to advance because it opens lines for White's other Bishop and doesn't damage the pawns on the Kingside. But Black has powerful trumps, especially the use of the open d-file after 11 d4 exd3, and the thrust of the Black c-pawn. Whatever defensive formation White adopts must include a way to meet ... c6-c5-c4. After 11 d4 exd3 12 ♘xd3 the poor besieged Knight on d3 may eventually be attacked by the c-pawn, and now the Knight has fewer places to go. Even if it finds a haven (e1, for example), Black will continue with ... ♗b7 and ... ♖ad8 with tremendous pressure along the d-file and the long diagonals leading to White's Kingside.

The continuation 11 d4 exd3 12 ♘xd3 ♕c7! 13 h3 0-0 14 b3!? looks like it leads to chances for both players. White can play ♗b2 and either ♘c3 or ♘a3 (both of which threaten ♘b5xd6 if Black plays ... c6-c5). If White can eliminate one of his opponent's attacking Bishops and castle safely, he will have excellent winning chances. After all, he's a pawn ahead.

Black, of course, is not to be counted out. He has the two central files for his Rooks and those two

diagonals (b7-g2 and d6-h2) for his Bishops. He also has d5, an excellent outpost for one of his Knights, and after he advances his c-pawn he will be able to reposition the other Knight with ... ♘c6-d4!.

All of what we have just said about Black's development also applies after 11 f4. Whenever your opponent has sacrificed a pawn you should always be on the lookout for opportunities to give it back in return for an advantage of at least equal value in some other form. After 11 f4 ♕c7 it would be hard for White to keep the extra pawn without incurring serious weaknesses (12 d4 exd3 13 ♘xd3 is worse now for White than in the 11 d4 line, because f2-f4 has merely damaged his own position). But White doesn't have to defend his threatened Knight—after 11 ... ♕c7 he can return the extra pawn with 12 0-0!, and after 12 ... ♗xe5 13 fxe5 ♕xe5 14 d4! he has a solid lead in development in exchange for the extra material. He also has an excellent dark-square Bishop—and Black doesn't. For example, after 14 ... ♕e7 15 ♕e1! (attacks the Knight on a5) 15 ... ♘b7 16 ♕g3, Black is on the defensive (16 ... 0-0 17 ♗xh6). Black's position is not improved by 14 ... exd3 because 15 ♗xd3 followed by ♘c3 and ♗f4 will give White excellent piece play and opportunities to attack the Kingside or the weakened enemy c-pawn.

Therefore Black meets **11 f4** with the en passant capture **11 ... exf3,** and after **12 ♘xf3** this is the position.

Position after 11 f4 exf3 12 ♘xf3

For the masters, this is where the Two Knights Defense really starts. White has kept the pawn he won on move five but has made some concessions along the way. His Kingside is a bit vulnerable and, more important, his opponent will be able to seize open lines.

Black's counterplay is based on ... c6-c5 followed by ... ♘c6-d4 and the development of his Queen Rook and Queen Bishop. The impact of ... c6-c5 depends on White's d-pawn. If White plays d2-d4 and Black plays his c-pawn up a square, the position is certain to be opened—and this includes the diagonal leading to White's castled King at g1 as well as the file leading to White's Queen at d1. White must take care not to get into a bad pin along one of those lines.

If White plays d2-d3 instead (as in the second illustrative game), he invites ... c6-c5 and ... ♘c6-d4. This has an inhibiting effect on White's position, for if he takes the Knight on d4 with his own Knight he removes his best defensive piece from the Kingside, and if he plays c2-c3 to stop the Black Knight's transfer to d4 he invites an attack on the weakened d-pawn with ... ♗a6 or ... ♗f5 and ... ♖ad8.

In the following two model games we see different methods of defense by White. (The same player is Black in both games.) Even with a slight inaccuracy at move 13, Black still has a strong game in our first example. It is only when he tries too hard (17 ... ♘b4?) that his game declines seriously. In the second game White plays too defensively and soon has no position left to defend.

Instructive Game No. 1

White: J. Timman
Black: A. Bisguier

Sombor 1974

1	e4	e5
2	♘f3	♘c6
3	♗c4	♘f6
4	♘g5	

After 4 d3 the position drifts into the Guioco Piano. By protecting his e-pawn White takes the attack out of Black's counterattack, but he also mutes the tenor of the game. Without d2-d4 the "giuoco" (game) really is "piano" (quiet).

Other fourth moves are questionable. On 4 0-0 Black can simply grab the e-pawn; e.g., 4 ... ♘xe4 5 d4 and now 5 ... exd4 6 ♖e1 d5 transposes into a position we considered earlier (after 4 d4 exd4 5 0-0 ♘xe4) and found equal, while 5 ... d5! 6 ♗b5 ♗d7 7 ♗xc6 bxc6 8 ♘xe5 ♗d6 is excellent for Black, for he can always dissolve his pawn weaknesses with ... c6-c5. In such variations White often takes so much time to regain his sacrificed pawn that he ends up behind in development.

Finally, the natural move 4 ♘c3 *may* transpose into the Giuoco Piano if Black consents with 4 ... ♗c5. But Black can remove all danger from the position by playing 4 ... ♘xe4!, a trick based on 5 ♘xe4 d5. Black's intent with 4 ... ♘xe4 is to end up with a superior concentration of pawns in the center. This central superiority is clear after 5 ♗xf7 +? ♔xf7 6 ♘xe4 d5! 7 ♘eg5 + ♔e8 followed by ... e5-e4 or ... h7-h6, and it is also evident—though less so—after 5 ♘xe4 d5 6 ♗d3 dxe4 7 ♗xe4. White has to avoid situations like this, in which Black's pawn on e5 gives him a strong hold on the center while White cannot advance his d-pawn beyond d3.

4	...	d5
5	exd5	♘a5
6	♗b5 +	c6
7	dxc6	bxc6
8	♗e2	h6
9	♘f3	e4

10	♘e5	♗d6

As troublesome as the attacks on this Knight are, retreating it to a safer square, such as c4 or g4, is too risky. The chief drawback to those moves is that they allow Black to exchange off White's only developed pieces while saving time—that is, with threats and captures—and without conferring any additional piece activity on White (such as the extra development he derives from d2-d4).

In concrete terms, 11 ♘g4 is met by 11 ... ♘xg4! 12 ♗xg4 ♕h4! 13 ♗xc8 ♖xc8 14 ♕e2 0-0, and Black is fully developed while White is virtually undeveloped and cannot castle without creating weaknesses (15 0-0?? ♕xh2 mate). Black's major trump in this kind of position is the threat of ... f7-f5-f4-f3! which would take the White Kingside apart.

The Knight can also jump to c4, but there it allows Black to exchange off his Knight that has been out of play for several moves. The position after 11 ♘c4 ♘xc4 12 ♗xc4 ♘g4! followed by ... ♕h4! illustrates what happens when you have no pieces defending your King position. White will eventually have to play d2-d3, which will open the position at a more dangerous time; i.e., when Black has the superior piece play.

11	f4	exf3
12	♘xf3	0-0
13	d4	

13 ...   c5?!

This is a natural move in the sense that Black wants open lines for his Bishops and wants to resuscitate his Queen Knight by way of c6. But it allows White to avoid the greatest dangers of checkmate by exchanging Queens (14 dxc5 and 15 ♕xd8). True, the pieces remaining on the board will still give Black an advantage in activity. But it may not be enough to make up for his missing pawn.

For this reason, 13 ... ♕c7 suggests itself. Then, after White castles, Black can play ... c5 and ... ♖d8. But White will also gain some time by playing ♘c3, threatening to trade off a dangerous Black Bishop (after ... c6-c5) with ♘b5! and ♘xd6.

14   dxc5   ♗xc5
15   ♕xd8   ♖xd8
16   ♗d2!

This fine move gains time by attacking Black's Knight and

preparing to castle on the Queenside. With Queens on the board, 0-0-0 would be highly risky for White. But with the chance of mate now reduced, the ability to quickly mobilize his Queen Rook on the d-file is very useful to White.

16 c3, which threatens to win a piece with b2-b4, is dangerous because of 16 ... ♖e8! with the counterthreat of 17 ... ♗a6. For example, 17 ♔f1 ♖xe2! 18 ♔xe2 ♗a6+ 19 ♔d1 ♘g4 and Black has a wonderful attack, with ... ♘f2+ and ... ♖d8+ coming up. You *can* get mated in the endgame.

16   ...   ♘c6
17   ♘c3   ♘b4?

This looks inviting, but 17 ... ♘g4! is better. Black would then be threatening 18 ... ♘b4 (19 0-0-0 ♘f2!) as well as 18 ... ♗f2+ or 18 ... ♘e3.

18   0-0-0   ♗f5
19   ♘e1   ♘g4

White's position seems on the verge of collapse because of his several weaknesses (c2, f2, e3). But just now is when his game begins to flower as Black's pieces are pushed back.

20   a3!

Now 20 ... ♘f2 21 axb4 ♘xd1 23 ♘xd1 or 22 bxc5 gives White two minor pieces for a Rook.

20	...	♞c6
21	♘d3	♝b6

And here 21 ... ♝xd3 would work if White played 22 ♗xd3 ♞f2, but not if he saw 22 ♗xg4!.

22	h3!	♞e3
23	♗xe3	♝xe3 +
24	♔b1	♞d4
25	♗g4	♝g6!

White has weathered the storm and kept his extra pawn. The position remains difficult because Black's Bishops keep an ominous eye on the position around the White King. White's task is to exchange Rooks and/or minor pieces so that he can advance the Queenside pawns with the help of his King. Notice how long Black has retained the initiative even after misplaying the attack (at move 17).

26	♖he1	♝g5
27	♞e2!	h5
28	♞xd4	♖xd4

The trouble with 28 ... hxg4 is that White's Knights are suddenly powerful after 29 ♞e5!, which threatens ♞xg6.

29	♗f3	♖c8
30	♖e5!	f6?!

After 30 ... ♗f6 31 ♖a5 White threatens both the a-pawn and the h-pawn, but Black can complicate matters with 31 ... ♖dc4, using his Rooks and Bishops to their maximum efficiency (32 c3 ♖b8 threatening 33 ... ♖xc3).

31	♖d5!	♖xd5

Now 31 ... ♖dc4 can be met by 32 ♖xg5! and 33 ♗d5 +, with further exchanges to increase the significance of White's extra pawn.

32	♗xd5 +	♔h7
33	b4!	

Finally it is safe for White to advance his pawns with the aid of his King. He can play c2-c4 and ♔b2-b3 with a juggernaut of pawns on the Queenside.

The game, already won for White, continued this way: **33 ... ♝e3 34 c4 ♔h6 35 ♔b2 f5 36 ♞e5 f4 37 c5 ♝f5 38 ♞f7 + ♔g6 39 ♞d6! ♖c7 40 ♞xf5 ♔xf5 41 ♗f3 g6 42 ♖d5 + ♔f6 43 ♔c3 ♖e7 44 a4 and Black resigned** (because nothing can be done about ♔c4, b5, a5, and b6-b7).

Instructive Game No. 2

White: E. Paoli
Black: A. Bisguier

Norristown, Pennsylvania, 1973

1	e4	e5
2	♘f3	♘c6
3	♗c4	♘f6
4	♘g5	d5
5	exd5	♘a5
6	♗b5+	c6
7	dxc6	bxc6
8	♗e2	h6
9	♘f3	e4
10	♘e5	♗d6
11	f4	exf3
12	♘xf3	0-0
13	0-0	c5
14	♘c3	

Certainly there is some logic behind White's refusal to play d2-d4, a move which gives Black's Bishops so much scope and unleashes additional dangers along the b6-g1 diagonal. But White's attempt to keep the position semi-closed has minuses too. By opening the game

with d2-d4 White at least tries to challenge Black's pieces and to offer exchanges. With his plan of d2-d3 he prefers instead to batten down the hatches and accept less operating space.

14 ... ♘c6

Now it is too late for 15 d4 because of 15 ... cxd4 16 ♘xd4 ♘xd4! 17 ♕xd4?? ♗xh2+).

15	a3?!	♖e8
16	d3	♖b8

Black's moves are easy to understand. He puts his pieces on squares that will be the most useful however White continues. If White defends his b2 with b2-b3 and ♗b2 he invites the occupation of his e3 (by ... ♘g4-e3, for example).

17 ♕e1?

This explains 15 a3, without which Black could now play 17 ... ♘b4!. White may be thinking about ♕h4, to use his most powerful piece, the Queen, to defend his most valuable piece, the King.

17 ... ♘d4!

But this powerful move throws White's forces into disarray. White cannot meet the double threat to his c2 and the Bishop on e2 unless he either swallows his pride and plays 18 ♕d1 or gives back a pawn. Chess

38

players are rarely willing to make such an abject admission of error.

18 ♘xd4   cxd4

Now if the Knight retreats, Black wins material by adding to the attack against the Bishop on e2, pinned to White's Queen. For example, 19 ♘d1 ♛e7 20 ♖f2 ♘g4. This illustrates the impact of … ♘c6-d4 very clearly.

19	♘e4	♘xe4
20	dxe4	♖xe4
21	♛f2	

White has managed to avert the disaster to his pinned Bishop at e2, but now he must cope with the absence of his Knight from the defense of the Kingside. It seems his defense will not be very difficult because ♗d3! will push Black's Rook back and permit a subsequent ♗f4!. Once Black's Bishops are neutralized, White may stand better because he can attack Black's d-pawn with his Rooks. His first

threat—and his last—is 22 ♛xf7 + .

21 …   ♛c7

This simple move kills White's chances. Black can now win with a Kingside attack or with the threat of … d4-d3 and … ♗c5.

22 h3   ♗g3!

After 22 … d3 23 ♗xd3 ♗c5 24 ♗xe4 ♗xf2 + 25 ♖xf2 White loses his Queen, but the material difference is very slight (Rook, Bishop, and pawn are roughly equivalent to a Queen). Black's attack would be over and it would be difficult for him to win the game. His actual move is much better.

23	♛f3	♗b7
24	♛d3	

There is no rest for White's Queen. If he plays 24 ♗d3 Black rushes in with 24 … ♖e3, uncovering an attack on the Queen with his Bishop. Then 26 ♛f5 g6 would win; e.g., 27 ♛g4 ♗h2 + 28 ♔h1 ♖g3! or 27 ♛f6 ♗h2 + 28 ♔h1 ♖xh3! (with threats of 29 … ♗e5 + and 29 … ♗xg2 + 30 ♔xg2 ♛g3 + and mates). Black's Bishops are sheer murder in these lines.

24 …   ♖e6!

Now the threat is 25 … ♗a6!.

25 ♗g4   ♖g6

26 ♕d1

White seems to have been able to plug up all the dangerous lines. But still he is several moves away from completing his development, and Black will inevitably find the weakness in his armor.

26 ...   ♗e4!

Ironically, it is the Queenside, where White has his extra pawn, that collapses first. He has no time for 27 ♗f5 because that unplugs the g-file: 27 ... ♘h2+ 28 ♔h1 ♗xg2 mate.

27 ♕xd4   ♕xc2
28 ♕d2

28 ...   ♖xb2!

A wonderful move. White's undeveloped Bishop cannot protect both the Queen and the b-pawn (29 ♗xb2 ♕xd2). And after 29 ♕d8+ ♔h7 White has no way to meet the threat against g2.

29 ♕xc2   ♖xc2
30 ♗f3   ♗xf3
31 ♖xf3   ♗e5
White resigns

After White saves his Rook with 32 ♖b1 he will either be mated by 32 ... ♖gxg2+ 33 ♔h1 ♖h2+ 34 ♔g1 ♗d4+ 35 ♔f1 ♖h1 or lose material to 33 ♔f1 ♗d4 34 ♔e1 ♖g1+ 35 ♖f1 ♗f2+ or 35 ... ♗c3+.

Part Four
Four Knights Game

Andy Soltis

The Four Knights Game has the reputation of quiet, balanced play that often leads to draws. The reputation is deserved, but amateur players can often create exciting middlegame positions by taking slight risks. While the Four Knights has lost its place in grandmaster tournaments, it can still be a dangerous weapon against an unsuspecting opponent among club and casual players.

What tends the opening toward draws is the *symmetry* of the pawn and piece placement. In a typical position after eight moves or so, Black's side of the board seems to be a mirror image of White's. White has played e2-e4 and is likely to keep the position relatively closed with d2-d3. Black will probably follow suit with ... d7-d6 after he's played 1 ... e7-e5. Both players develop their Knights on their most natural squares—White's on c3 and f3, Black's on c6 and f6. Furthermore, White will build up an attack against Black's e-pawn with ♗b5, which threatens to undermine the pawn's support with ♗xc6. And the most solid way for Black to answer this threat is to put his own King Bishop on b4, so that

he can capture White's e-pawn after ... ♗xc3. The other pair of Bishops may also be part of the mirror image, with White's going to g5 while Black's goes to g4. And both players almost always castle on the Kingside.

Of course, this symmetry must be broken eventually. If Black simply imitates White's moves he will finally reach a position in which imitation is impossible (such as when White gives a check). Black will have to upset the balance along the way, and this may involve risks to him—in fact, the "safest" method of diverging from symmetry involves the sacrifice of a pawn. But the basic opening position is so evenly structured—because the pieces naturally match one another on their mirror-image squares—that it is as risky for White as it is for Black to avoid a drawish, dull position. Madcap attackers should look elsewhere.

The opening is characterized by:

White		Black
1	e4	e5
2	♘f3	♘c6
3	♘c3	♘f6

With his third move Black announces his intention to follow White's lead at least for the present. White has made no threats with his third move and Black has his first opportunity to avoid symmetry.

He can seize the opportunity by developing his King Bishop with 3 ... ♝b4 or 3 ... ♝c5 or preparing to develop it on the long diagonal with 3 ... g6. Of the three, 3 ... ♝c5 is the least attractive because White has a little tactical trick that enables him to obtain a superior pawn center. This is 4 ♘xe5!, to meet 4 ... ♘xe5 with 5 d4. Then, whether Black plays 5 ... ♝xd4 or 5 ... ♝d6 6 dxe5 ♝xe5, he will find that his e-pawn is gone and that White has the stronger pawn center. (A fuller discussion of this kind of center appears at the beginning of the next chapter, but here we can point out that White can use his d5-square as an outpost because of the pawn on e4, whereas Black has no comparable outpost.)

The problem with 3 ... ♝b4 is 4 ♘d5, threatening to capture a Bishop for a Knight. This exchange is almost always favorable for White when he can open the position later on (with d2-d4, for example) because in an open position the Bishop's range exceeds the Knight's. After 4 ♘d5 Black can retreat his Bishop to a5 or e7, but either move is an admission that Black has lost time which has permitted White to plant his Knight on an excellent central square. White may use this gain of time to seize the momentum in the center, such as with 4 ... ♝e7 4 d4! d6 5 ♝b5. Then the pressure on Black's e-pawn may force him into a somewhat passive position with 6 ... exd4 7 ♘xd4 ♝d7.

Or, to avoid the loss of time, Black can concede the slight advantage of Bishop-vs.-Knight. But 4 ♘d5 ♘f6, for example, leads to a relatively simple position in which, after 5 ♘xb4 ♘xb4 6 ♘xe5 d6 7 ♘f3 ♘xe4 8 c3 followed by d2-d4, White's Bishop gives him a small but clear advantage.

Black's best bet for an alternative third move is 3 ... g6, followed by ... ♝g7, ... ♘ge7, and ... 0-0 if possible. This setup of pieces would stop White from playing d2-d4 and would protect Black's e-pawn. Black could continue in the middlegame with ... d7-d6, ... ♝e6 (or ... ♝g4), and ... f7-f5 with a potential Kingside assault.

White can shake up Black's plans with an immediate 4 d4 exd4 5 ♘d5! because of a little trap. If

Black continues routinely with 5 ... ♗g7 6 ♗g5 ♘ge7 White plays 7 ♘xd4! (threatening to win a piece with 8 ♘xc6 and 9 ♗xe7) 7 ... ♗xd4? 8 ♕xd4!! ♘xd4 9 ♘f6+ and 10 ♗h6 mate. No better is 6 ... ♘f6 7 e5!.

But this excitement in the center is short-lived if Black plays 6 ... ♘ce7! instead of 6 ... ♘ge7 or 6 ... ♘f6. Black would welcome an exchange of Knights on e7 because he could then continue his plan of bearing down along the diagonal leading from his g7 to d4 and c3. If White plays 7 ♘xd4 c6! 8 ♘c3 (to avoid exchanges that would ease Black's restricted position), Black can eliminate White's claim to pawn superiority in the center with 8 ... h6 9 ♗f4 d5!. Once Black safely achieves ... d7-d5 in this position, White's bridgehead at e4 will be dissolved and his pieces will have no superiority in terms of central outposts. In 1 e4 e5 games the move ... d7-d5 is often regarded as "The Old Equalizer."

4 ♗b5

Aside from 4 d4, which we'll consider in the notes to the illustrative game and which may transpose into the opening discussed in the next chapter, the only fourth move dangerous to Black is 4 ♗b5, threatening to win a pawn with 5 ♗xc6 and 6 ♘xe5.

At first glance, 4 ♗c4 seems worth a try. But it permits the same kind of tactical trick we saw in 3 ... ♗c5 4 ♘xe5. This time it is Black who can upset the center with 4 ♗c4 ♘xe4! 5 ♘xe4 d5, after which he will have a good e-pawn in the center to support his pieces and White's will have been dissolved.

After 4 ♗c4 ♘xe4 beginners are often attracted to 5 ♗xf7+. Since White is going to lose his temporary material advantage of a Knight in one move anyway, why not give it up by disrupting Black's King? The answer is that the Black King will be perfectly safe once White gives up his Bishop and his pawn control of the center with 5 ♗xf7+ ♔xf7 6 ♘xe4 d5. Black's loss of the castling privilege is of minor importance because his King is quite safe after, say, 7 ♘eg5+ ♔g8 and 8 ... h6! followed by ... ♔h7 and ... ♖f8. But Black's powerful pawn center is something that won't go away. After 4 ♗c4 ♘xe4! Black stands comfortably better after 5 ♗xf7+? and equalizes easily after 5 ♘xe4.

4 ...   ♘d4!?

This is the distinctive move of the modern Four Knights Game, replacing the older favorite, 4 ... ♗b4. The Bishop move was popular until the first World War and then faded from master play because of the equalizing strength of 4 ... ♘d4. Yet Black can still obtain an adequate—and more enterprising—position with 4 ... ♗b4 if he plays carefully following 5 0-0 0-0 6 d3 d6 7 ♗g5, the symmetrical variation.

**After 4 ... ♗b4 5 0-0 0-0
6 d3 d6 7 ♗g5**

Eventually Black must stop his policy of imitation. For example, 7 ... ♗g4 8 ♘d5! ♘d4 9 ♘xb4 ♘xb5 10 ♘d5 ♘d4 11 ♕d2! punishes Black because he cannot meet the threat of 12 ♗xf6 gxf6 13 ♕h6 and 14 ♘xf6+ by playing the same moves. At some point White will give a check which Black cannot legally ignore by giving an imitative check of his own (for instance, 11 ♕d2 ♕d7 12 ♘xf6+ gxf6 13 ♗xf6 and 14 ♕g5+).

In the diagram we see that White is threatening to mount a Kingside attack: ♘d5 followed by a capture on f6 would disrupt the pawns around Black's King. The easiest answer to the ♘d5 threat is simply 7... ♗xc3!, eliminating the Knight. Then after 8 bxc3 Black still faces a problem because of the pin on his Knight at f6. He can wriggle out of the pin with the "Metger Unpin," a clever idea named for the analyst who discovered it at the turn of the century.

Black plays 8 ... ♕e7 followed by ... ♘d8 and ... ♘e6. If White then retreats his Bishop along the c1-g5 diagonal, Black can continue with ... ♘c5 and create a pin of his own with ... ♗g4. If White retreats his Bishop to h4 when it is attacked by ... ♘e6, Black can break the pin once and for all with ... ♘f4 followed by ... ♘g6 and (if necessary) ... h6. There is no way the White Bishop can maintain the pin after that. For instance, 8 ... ♕e7 9 ♖e1 ♘d8 10 d4 ♘e6 11 ♗h4 ♘f4 12 ♕d2 ♘g6.

After this kind of play Black stands well because of his rock-solid position. If White plays d3-d4 at some point—and this is the main method for him to open the position for his Bishops and Rooks—Black can build a pawn structure on the dark squares. That is, he will put pawns at c5 and d6.

Then White's dark-square Bishop will not have a great impact on Black's position because it will "bite on granite"—the granite of Black pawns.

And while all this is happening, Black can also play ... ♗d7 and ... ♖ac8 so that he can exchange pawns at the right moment and use his Rook along the c-file. White can avert this by playing d4-d5, but that closes the position—something you don't want to do when you have Bishops because they are long-range pieces—and gives Black an excellent counterattacking chance with ... ♞e8 and ... f5.

In contrast to the closed positional struggle that follows 4 ... ♗b4, there is an open (and for Black unappetizing) middlegame after the inferior 4 ... ♗c5. White can once again use the trick of a pawn fork (♞xe5 and d2-d4) to gain the upper hand in the center. The best way to do it is **5 0-0** and, if 5 ... 0-0, then 6 ♞xe5! ♞xe5 7 d4 ♗d6 8 f4! ♞c6 9 e5, and eventually White gets his minor piece back and has a powerful advantage because he controls more space in the center of the board (e.g., 9 ... ♗b4 10 d5!).

Black can avoid the tactical trick after 5 0-0 by playing 5 ... d6, but then 6 d4! permits White to advance his pieces in the center and destroys the strong Black e-pawn; e.g., 6 ... exd4 7 ♞xd4 ♗d7 9 ♞f5 ♗xf5 10 exf5 followed by ♗g5 and

either ♞d5 or ♞e4 with a strong Kingside attack.

Position after 4 ... ♞d4

The power of Black's 4 ... ♞d4 stems from the disruptive effect it has on White's pieces. The Knight now attacks not only the White Bishop (b5) but also the Knight (f3) that is the key to the attack on Black's e-pawn. If the Black Knight is captured (5 ♞xd4 exd4) White's Bishop loses its threat on b5 and White's other Knight is under attack.

5 ♞xd4

This is the safest method of proceeding, but it leads to a middlegame so deadly even that it will take several errors for either side to lose. Since Black has taken some risks with 4 ... ♞d4, it is fair to ask whether White can take some in order to extract an advantage from the position. After all, Black has moved an already developed piece for the second time (... ♘b8-c6-d4) before moving either of his Bishops. White has three pieces developed compared with Black's two, and he has the move. What can he do with it?

The most obvious effort to refute 4 ... ♘d4 is to take what has been left unguarded: **5 ♘xe5.** If Black regains material equality with 5 ... ♘xb5 and 6 ... ♘xe4, White will answer powerfully with 7 ♕e2! (7 ... ♘f6? 8 ♘c6 discovered check or 7 ... d5 8 d3). But White's use of the e-file in this last line suggests that Black can anticipate him with **5 ... ♕e7!** (instead of 5 ... ♘xb5). Then, if 6 ♘f3 ♘xb5 7 ♘xb5 ♕xe4+ 8 ♕e2 ♕xe2+, Black has a slight endgame advantage in the form of a more mobile Bishop against a Knight.

If White is going to try 5 ♘xe5 he must be prepared to answer 5 ... ♕e7 with **6 f4!?.** That allows him to avoid the exchange of Queens with 6 ... ♘xb5 7 ♘xb5 d6 8 ♘f3 ♕xe4+ 9 ♔f2, threatening to repulse Black's momentum with 10 ♖e1 winning the Queen, or 10 ♘xc7+ forking King and Rook. The position becomes very tactical after 9 ... ♘g4+ 10 ♔g1 ♕c6! 11 ♕e2+ ♗e7 or 10 ♔g3 ♕g6! (threatening a discovered check) 11 ♘h4 ♕h5 12 h3 ♘f6 13 ♕xh5 ♘xh5+, which leads to an equal position. It also avoids two traps: 12 ♘xc7+ ♔d8 and now 13 ♘xa8 g5! 14 fxg5 ♕xg5 followed by a decisive discovered check, or 13 h3

♘f6 14 ♘xa8 ♕xh4+!! 15 ♔xh4 ♘e4 and 16 ... ♗e7 followed by mate.

White can also retreat his Bishop at move five to avoid 5 ... ♘xb5. It seems most natural to bring it back to c4, but that permits Black to move his d-pawn. Black may equalize with the solid **5 ♗c4** ♘xf3+ 6 ♕xf3 d6 followed by developing his Bishops on e6 and e7, or he can try the more adventurous 5 ... ♗c5 6 ♘xe5 ♕e7 7 ♘f3 (or 7 ♘d3) d5!. In this last line, for instance, Black gets wonderful compensation for a sacrificed pawn in the form of active attacking Bishops (7 ♘d3 d5 8 ♗xd5 ♘xd5 9 ♘xd5 ♕xe4+ 10 ♘e3 ♗d6 11 0-0 ♗e6 and 12 ... 0-0-0!).

The best chance for White to enliven the game and still avoid any serious risk of losing is **5 ♗a4!?.** This averts 5 ... ♘xb5 and renews the threat to capture Black's e-pawn, and since the Bishop is still on the a4-e8 diagonal, Black can play neither ... d7-d6 to defend his e-pawn nor ... d7-d5 as a followup to the sacrifice of the e-pawn.

The immobility of Black's d-pawn is significant after 5 ... ♘xf3+ 6 ♕xf3 because 6 ... ♗e7? permits White to attack both the e-pawn and the g-pawn with 7 ♕g3!. Black would have to take the time for 6 ... c6 and 7 ... d6 before developing his King Bishop. Also, if Black sacrifices his e-pawn, the impossibility of ...

d7-d5 takes away much of his momentum. For example, 5 ... ♝c5 6 ♞xe5 ♛e7 7 ♞d3 is more effective for White than when his Bishop is on c4 because 7 ... d5 is illegal and 7 ... ♞xe4 8 0-0! leaves Black far behind in development (8 ... ♞xc3 9 dxc3 ♞e6 10 ♞xc5 ♛xc5 11 ♝e3).

Black's best bet in this sacrifice line is to forget about immediately regaining his pawn. Instead, he should play **5 ... ♝c5 6 ♞xe5 0-0.**

After 5 ♝a4 ♝c5 6 ♞xe5 0-0

Now Black really does threaten to play ... d5, a move that would open the center just when White's pieces and his King are vulnerable to harassment. For instance, 7 d3 d5! would prepare 8 ... ♛e7, after which 9 ♝f4 would walk into 9 ... ♝d6 (winning material because of the pin on the Knight) and 9 f4 would make it unwise for White to castle for several moves in view of a possible check uncovered by a move of Black's Knight from d4.

Position after 5 ♞xd4

| 5 | ... | exd4 |
| 6 | e5 | |

White's hand is forced now because alternatives such as 6 ♞e2 and 6 ♞b1 permit simply 6 ... ♞xe4, after which Black can develop comfortably with ... c6, ... d5, and ... ♝d6 or ... ♝e7.

| 6 | ... | dxc3 |

Black's hand is forced also. His Knight has no good retreat.

| 7 | exf6 | ♛xf6! |

As long as a series of captures is in progress, neither player wants to be caught short—as in a game of musical chairs when the music stops. White is running second in the series that began with 6 ... dxc3; that is, he captured a Knight after Black did and will capture a pawn after Black does. Black can upset the series by playing 7 ... cxd2 with check, and after White recaptures on d2, Black captures on f6 and the series ends with Black a pawn ahead.

But it's not so easy. After 7 ... cxd2+ 8 ♗xd2 ♛xf6 White is ahead in development to the extent of both Bishops, and it is his turn to move again. With 9 0-0 he has more than enough compensation for his pawn in view of the good Bishop diagonals and his easy access to the e-file. For example, 9 ... ♗e7 10 ♗c3 ♛g5 11 ♖e1! and now 11 ... ♛xb5 12 ♛g4, threatening ♛xg7 and then ♗f6, would be too strong for Black to handle (12 ... ♖g8 13 ♗f6!). Similarly, 11 ... 0-0 is too risky because of 12 ♖e5!, after which Black's Queen may be separated from the defense of his Bishop.

8 dxc3

8 bxc3 divides White's pawns into three groups, which makes them slightly weaker than after 8 dxc3. Even so, the position is still very balanced after 8 ... c6! 9 ♗a4 ♛e5+. But Black can get some winning chances with 9 ... d5! instead.

8 ...   ♛e5+

If Black resists the temptation to exchange Queens, White may insist: 8 ... ♗c5 9 ♛e2+ ♛e6 10 ♗c4!. Or White can play 9 0-0, threatening 10 ♖e1+ ♗e7 11 ♛e2 which would stop Black from castling. If Black plays 9 ... 0-0, then after 10 ♗xd7!

♖d8 11 ♛h5 ♗xd7 12 ♛xc5 White cannot be considered worse.

9 ♛e2   ♛xe2+
10 ♗xe2

Now we see the fruits of caution. The dead even position is once again approaching symmetry and is almost surely headed for a draw. The absence of Queens means that it will be extremely hard for either side to develop a mating attack against the enemy King and that the game will be decided by endgame advantages. But here there are no such advantages of any significance—no superior Bishops, Rooks, or Kings. True, White has doubled pawns on the c-file, but they are not easy to attack. Moreover, White's four Queenside pawns balance Black's four pawns, so neither side will be able to create a passed pawn (an endgame advantage) without resorting to extraordinary means.

In fact, this position is almost always a prelude to a draw in master chess. One of the few grandmaster games that continued to be a fight went 10 ... d5 11 ♗e3 ♗d6 12 0-0 0-0 13 ♖fe1 ♗f5 14 ♗d3! ♗xd3 15 cxd3 ♖fe8 16 ♗d2, but soon all the Rooks were exchanged and a draw was agreed.

Moral: The Four Knights is so evenly balanced that even a superior player cannot expect to win regularly with it. Akiba Rubinstein, the great Polish grandmaster, is often credited (incorrectly, it seems) with inventing 4 ... ♘d4. But Rubinstein eventually gave up on 4 ... ♘d4 because of the inevitability of drawish positions after 5 ♘xd4, and returned to 4 ... ♗b4, which is probably Black's best way of trying to avoid a draw. White, on the other hand, can sharpen play by not answering 4 ... ♘d4 with 5 ♘xd4.

Instructive Game

White: N. Gaprindashvili
Black: A. Kushnir

Women's World Championship
Match, Riga 1965

1	e4	e5
2	♘f3	♘c6
3	♘c3	♘f6
4	♗b5	

One important escape from the balanced nature of the Four Knights is 4 d4. Then 4 ... exd4 would permit White to transpose—that is, to guide the position by an alternate move order—into the Scotch Game (discussed in the next chapter).

Also, both White and Black have ways of avoiding the normal Scotch Game after 4 d4.

Black's method is **4 d4 ♗b4!?**. This puts immediate pressure on White's center with the threat of 5 ... ♘xe4. After 5 d5 ♘e7 6 ♘xe5 d6 Black will regain his pawn with a fine game after ... ♘xe4. The position can become more complicated after the immediate 5 ♘xe5, but even then Black may equalize with 5 ... ♘xe4 or with the more ambitious 5 ... 0-0, delaying the capture of the e-pawn and planning to play ... ♖e8 or ... ♕e7. But there is plenty of fight.

White's method of shaking up the chances comes after **4 d4 exd4** and now **5 ♘d5**. This, the Belgrade Gambit, leads to immense complications if Black accepts a second pawn with 5 ... ♘xe4 6 ♕e2 f5 7 ♘g5. It is much safer for Black to play 5 ... ♗e7 followed by castling. For example, 6 ♗f4 (threatening to take on c7) 6 ... d6 7 ♘xd4 ♘xd4 8 ♕xd4 ♘xd5 and ... ♗f6 is quite equal. And if White takes the time to play ♘xe7 to gain the advantage of Bishop against Knight, then at some point after ... ♕xe7 he will have difficulty protecting his e-pawn.

| 4 | ... | ♘d4 |
| 5 | ♗a4 | |

This is White's best bid for a slight edge in what is likely to end up as a nearly symmetrical position. White hopes Black will respond to the threat of 6 ♘xe5 by exchanging Knights with 5 ... ♘xf3+. This would permit White to save time by recapturing on f3 with her Queen, which may later be powerfully posted on g3 where it attacks g7. By exchanging Knights with 5 ... ♘xf3+ Black would further White's development but not her own.

5	...	♗c5
6	0-0	

This is relatively conservative (compared to 6 ♘xe5) but more adventurous than the series of exchanges that would probably result from 5 ♘xd4. White wants to get her pieces developed with 0-0, d2-d3, and ♗g5 without upsetting the center. Perhaps a later exchange of Knights in the center will be more useful to White's development.

6	...	0-0
7	d3	c6!?

Black isn't willing to accept an inferior position in which only White makes threats. With her last move Black prepares ... d7-d5 and also

keeps enemy pieces off d5. This is important if you look at 7 ... d6, the normal move. Then 8 ♘xd4 ♗xd4 9 ♗g5 creates a threat of 10 ♘d5 with its powerful pressure on f6. (Black can play 8 ... exd4, but after 9 ♘e2 Black's Bishop is sharply reduced in effectiveness.)

8 ♘xd4

Black's e-pawn has been hanging in the air without visible means of support for four moves now. But the hidden means are enough to stop ♘xe5, which would be met now by 8 ... d6! and if 9 ♘c4 then 9 ... b5, winning a piece by forking Bishop and Knight. White saves his piece if he plays 9 ♘f3 instead, but then 9 ... ♗g4! creates a dangerous position for White in which it will be difficult for him to untangle his Kingside pieces because his Queen must keep protecting f3. For example, 10 ♕e1? ♗xf3! wins material, and 10 ♗e3 ♗xf3 11 gxf3 ♘h5 gives Black strong pressure against the squares g2, f3, and f4 after 12 ... ♕f6 or 12 ... ♕h4.

8 ... ♗xd4

A case can be made for 8 ... exd4 if it is followed up with ... d7-d5; e.g., 8 ... exd4 9 ♘e2 d5 10 exd5 ♘xd5 and Black's Bishop on c5 can gain a better life later at d6.

9	♘e2!	♗b6
10	♗g5	h6

11	&h4	d6
12	&h1!	

White has used her quiet opening play to set up a problem for Black on the Kingside. Now it is Black who cannot safely get out of the attack on her Knight (12 ... &c7 13 &xf6! followed by &g3 and &h5). This impediment to Black's development will become more serious if White can add to the pressure against f6 by playing f2-f4 and opening the f-file. This is why White played &h1, vacating the diagonal from b6 to g1 that is watched by Black's Bishop.

12	...	g5

So much for f2-f4. But this adds a significant weakness to Black's King position. White can play f2-f3 and then d2-d4 followed by the opening of the d-file. White can also exploit the "holes" created by Black's last move by swinging her Knight to g3 and from there to h5 or f5. (Holes are squares that can no longer be protected by pawns.)

13	&g3	&h5
14	d4!	&f4!

This is much better than 14 ... &xg3+, which would remove Black's only good defensive piece on the Kingside while not cutting down White's attacking potential. White would recapture on g3 with her h-pawn (so she can meet ... &g4 with f2-f3) and prepare to assault the Kingside with &b3, c2-c3, &d2, and f2-f4.

15	c3	&f6

Black can win a pawn with 15 ... &xe2+ 16 &xe2 exd4. But that opens the game in a sector of the board where she is not ready for hand-to-hand combat. After 17 &ad1 dxc3 18 &xd6 or 17 ... &f6 18 e5! White's better developed pieces run riot in the center.

16	f3!	&h7
17	&f2	&g8

Black has carefully kept the center closed while taking steps to minimize the danger when it is opened. She does not fear an exchange of pawns on e5 because White can't do much with the d-file yet. And she doesn't fear &xf4 because Black would then get some play along the g-file after ... gxf4.

But White has been just as careful. She has reinforced her d-pawn and is ready to work on those h5 and f5 holes we mentioned a few moves ago. She will play ♘g3 and then work up something along the d-file with ♕d2 and ♖ad1. Then, after an exchange of pawns on e5, she can play ♕d6!, gaining space for her pieces. To avert this, Black begins an attack on the Kingside that turns out to be ill-advised.

18	♘g3	g4?
19	♗e3!	♕h4
20	♕d2	

Suddenly White has taken over the momentum on the Kingside with her own threats (♗xf4 being the most important one). Black is committed to attack now because retreats will only expose her Kingside to counterattack; e.g., 20 ... ♘h5 21 ♘xh5 ♕xh5 22 fxg4! ♗xg4 23 ♖f6!.

20	...	♗e6
21	♗xf4	exf4
22	♕xf4	

White has won a pawn and has also eliminated Black's strongest point in the center, e5. White is not thinking only about an endgame in which her extra pawn will count; she would just as soon give mate in the middlegame with e4-e5 and ♗c2+. The rest of the game is a slaughter: **22 ... ♗d8 23 ♗c2! ♗g5 24 e5+ ♔g7 25 ♕e4 gxf3 26 ♕xf3 ♔g4? 27 ♕xg4 ♗xg4 28 ♗f5! h5 29 ♗xg4 hxg4 30 ♘f5+ ♔g6 31 ♘xd6 ♖h8? 32 ♘xf7, Black resigned.**

Part Five
Scotch Game

Andy Soltis

Of the openings that begin 1 e4 e5, the Scotch Game is the purest example of White's attempt to dominate the center. His strategy is to assault the Black e-pawn directly and immediately and force Black to trade off his important anchor-pawn in the center. This opening strategy differs from that of other 1 e4 e5 openings. In the Ruy Lopez and the Four Knights Game, for example, White seeks to win the Black e-pawn with his pieces. In the Two Knights Defense and the Giuoco Piano, White tries to exploit squares that have been weakened by the advance 1 ... e5, especially d5, f5, and f7. But in the Scotch, White decides to *liquidate* Black's e-pawn—that is, to force Black to trade it for White's d-pawn—so that White may open the center for his pieces and profit from the fact that Black no longer has a foothold in the center.

The diagram shows the pawn structure after the first four moves.

This skeleton of pawns favors White slightly. Why? Well, let's consider where the two sides will place their pieces. White has a pawn in the center and Black does not. This fact permits White easily

to occupy d5, the square protected by his e-pawn. A Knight will be ideal on d5, where it attacks Black's pawn at c7, watches the Kingside squares e7 and f6, and is generally a nuisance to Black. The d5-square is also quite suitable for a Bishop or a Rook. The square f5 is another useful outpost for White's pieces—especially for a Knight, which can watch the Kingside from that powerful protected outpost.

Moreover, these outposts can be safely maintained until Black decides to play ... c7-c6 or ... g7-g6. If and when either of those moves is made, White will revise his strategy and begin to exploit Black's new weaknesses. For example, ... c7-c6 relinquishes

Black's last remaining pawn protection of the d6-square. This means that White can try to occupy that square, blocking up Black's center and obstructing the development of his Bishop. Or, if Black plays ... d7-d6 *and* ... c7-c6, the d-pawn will be a natural target for White's pieces (♗f4, ♖ad1), and it can no longer be protected by a pawn.

The favorable nature of this pawn structure for White means that Black has the task of freeing himself and avoiding what can easily become a passive, painful middlegame.

White	Black
1 e4	e5
2 ♘f3	♘c6
3 d4	

White's third move identifies the Scotch Game. It virtually forces Black to liquidate his newly established pawn center. His pawn at e5 can be maintained only by supporting it with another pawn, say 3 ... d6. But that move is frowned upon because White can force

matters with 4 dxe5 dxe5 5 ♕xd8+ ♔xd8 (5 ... ♘xd8 6 ♘xe5!) and 6 ♗c4 or 6 ♘c3. He will then castle eventually on the Queenside, and enjoy a large lead in development.

3	...	exd4
4	♘xd4	

By recapturing with his Knight, White places one of his pieces where it will be most useful—in the center, where it watches several key squares (b5, c6, e6, and f5). Already it gives Black a problem, for the Knight denies his Queen Bishop its best squares. And Black can remove that powerful piece only if he is willing to accept an even more powerful White piece in the center—the Queen—after 4 ... ♘xd4? 5 ♕xd4.

But Black does have ways of dealing with White's strategy in the center. Before examining them, we will look at a sharp alternative for White on his fourth move. Instead of the natural and logical 4 ♘xd4, White can turn the game in more tactical directions with **4 c3!?**.

The Göring Gambit

This introduces an offshoot of the Scotch Game called the Göring Gambit. White sacrifices a pawn to break open the d- and c-files, and he keeps his Knight at f3 so that it can be used to assault f7 by way of e5 or g5. White may give his primary attention to the Kingside, but he is also ready to adopt a strategy of keeping Black's pieces in passive positions by paying more attention to the center and the Queenside. For example, with Rooks on c1 and d1 and a Knight on d5 he will have a ready-made attack on c7. If Black moves his c-pawn, then the d-pawn becomes the target. By forcing Black's pieces to defend these weaknesses, White hopes to stretch the defense to the breaking point.

After **4 ... dxc3** White can build a harmonious battlefront with **5 ♘xc3** and then ♗c4, ♕b3, and ♗g5. For example, **5 ... ♗c5 6 ♗c4 d6 7 ♗g5!** poses serious problems for Black. His Bishop on c5 shields the target at c7, but, having been shut out of the Kingside by ... d7-d6, the Bishop can no longer be used for defense there. So after 7 ♗g5 Black has the choice of weakening his pawns with either 7 ... f6 or 7 ... ♘f6 (which would be met by 8 ♘d5). Black can avoid both of those weakening moves by playing 7 ... ♘ge7, but his pieces will be passively posted after 8 ♘d5.

In these and similar positions the White Knight at d5 commands a great deal of respect. For this reason, the best line of defense for Black is believed to begin with **5 ... ♗b4**

(instead of 5 ... ♗c5), to pin that Knight before it can go to d5, or perhaps to capture it on c3. Ordinarily, Black would not want to give up such a fine Bishop merely to keep a White Knight out of d5. But since Black is a pawn ahead he is willing to make a concession, and giving up a Bishop for a Knight is not at all hard to live with.

A typical example of accurate defense by Black is 5 ... ♗b4 6 ♗c4 d6 7 0-0 ♗xc3! (otherwise 8 ♘d5!) 8 bxc3 ♗e6. This procedure neutralizes White's most dangerous minor pieces—his light-square Bishop and his Queen Knight. White's other Bishop is a good piece, to be sure, but it does not enjoy an unobstructed diagonal as it would like to do. Also, White's Rooks do not have a convenient target since the d-file is plugged by Black's pawn on d6 (which is protected by a fellow pawn on c7).

If Black manages to castle on the Kingside he will have an excellent game—even if White regains his pawn. For example, after 8 ... ♗e6 if White continues 9 ♗xe6 fxe6 10 ♕b3, Black can mobilize his pieces to maximum efficiency with 10 ... ♕d7! 11 ♕xb7 ♖b8 12 ♕a6 ♘ge7 13 ♗g5 0-0. Then he will take control of the open file with ... ♖b6 and ♖fb8, or attack on the Kingside with ... ♘g6-f4.

There are two ways of viewing such a result. It shows either that White should play less adventurously—i.e., not sacrifice a pawn with 4 c3!?—or that he should play *more* adventurously and sacrifice *two* pawns! For example, after 4 ... dxc3 he can play **5 ♗c4?!**.

Göring Gambit after 5 ♗c4

This gives White more immediate threats, especially against f7. For example, 5 ... ♗e7? runs into 6 ♕d5! ♘h6 7 ♗xh6. But Black can safely grab the second pawn and, if he is careful, can live happily into the middlegame and, even better, the endgame.

After **5 ... cxb2 6 ♗xb2** White's Bishops appear to rake the Kingside. Yet after **6 ... d6!** they will be blunted and Black will stand well. He can meet a concerted attack on his f7 by playing ... ♕d7 and ... ♘d8; e.g., on 7 ♕b3 ♕d7! Black threatens to trade off White's attacking Bishop with 8 ... ♘a5!. As for the other Bishop, Black must be careful to

play ... ♘f6 and block the long b2-g7 diagonal before he moves his King Bishop from the defense of g7. But once he has played ... ♘f6 and ... ♗e7, he can castle serenely on the Kingside and be ready to challenge White's dark-square Bishop with ... ♘d7 and ... ♗f6.

The best try for White after 6 ... d6! is **7 0-0**, hoping to get steady pressure against Black's pieces and to open lines with a timely e4-e5!. But Black again neutralizes the dangerous attack on his f7 with **7 ... ♗e6!**. White can't afford to lose time with 8 ♗b5 because he is two pawns down and must develop some kind of meaningful attack before Black castles and exploits his material advantage. Moreover, White can't even win back one of his pawns with 8 ♗xe6 fxe6 9 ♕b3 ♕d7! 10 ♕xb7—as he can in the 5 ♘xc3 variation—because 10 ... ♖b8! wins the Bishop on b2 after White retreats his Queen.

Instead, White must try to open the position for his temporarily more active pieces with 10 ♘g5 ♘d8! 11 f4 and then f4-f5 or e4-e5. But with 11 ... ♘f6 12 f5 e5! or 12 e5 dxe5 13 fxe5 ♘d5 Black keeps the position relatively blocked, and his two-pawn advantage should count eventually.

Of course, there are other ways for Black to answer the Göring Gambit (such as declining it with 4 ... d3 or 4 ... d5 or 4 ... ♘f6), but this gambit well illustrates an old chess maxim: The best way to refute a gambit is to accept it.

Meanwhile, back at **4 ♘xd4** ...

Here White has the benefits of the superior pawn structure we mentioned earlier, and he did not have to sacrifice material to get them. He is ready to develop his King Bishop at c4 and castle quickly. When his e-pawn is attacked he will defend it with ♘c3. Then, after he posts his other Bishop at either g5, f4, or e3, he will be able to continue with ♕d2 and ♖ad1, achieving a fine concentration of pieces in the center. To shake up Black's position he can proceed either with f2-f4 and e4-e5 or with ♘d5.

Black has three different ways of meeting this plan. He can challenge White's pieces by rapidly developing his own pieces. He can try to interfere with White's development with harassing threats. Or he can exploit White's own weakness, his e-pawn, before White can conveniently protect it.

4 ...   ♘f6!

This combines the best aspects of development, harassment, and exploitation of the e-pawn. It also leads to very sharp play, and some players may want to consider the chief alternatives. They are:

a) **4 ... ♗c5.** This has been traditionally the most popular response. He brings out another piece while saving time by attacking the White Knight. If the Knight retreats to b3 Black will have to spend a move to retreat his attacked Bishop, but at least he will have removed the dangerous centralized Knight from d4. Another Knight move, 5 ♘xc6, simply accedes to Black's wishes and gives him a fine pawn center after 5 ... bxc6 and ... d7-d5.

More promising is 5 ♗e3, matching Black's developing move with a White developing move and also making a threat: 6 ♘xc6! bxc6 7 ♗xc5, or if 6 ... ♗xe3?? 7 ♘xd8. But 5 ♗e3 gives Black time for 5 ... ♕f6! 6 c3 ♘ge7. Black then has a slight lead in development—three minor pieces developed to White's two—and is ready to increase the margin. White will find it difficult to develop smoothly because of the pressure on his d4. For example, he can't move his King Bishop to d3 because it would block his Queen and thereby lose a pawn to 7 ... ♘xd4. And he can't move his Knight from d4—except to the passive c2-square—without having his pawn structure ruptured. For instance, 7 ♘b3 is now a poor move: 7 ... ♗xe3 8 fxe3 grants Black an outpost at e5 that will prove highly valuable for

57

his Knights and also weakens the squares around White's King. Finally, White cannot develop his Bishop on e2 or g2 (after 7 g3, for instance) without allowing 7 ... d5!, which eliminates the pawn center that White was hoping would carry him favorably into the middlegame. (And if White plays 7 ♗c4 to stop 7 ... d5, Black gains time with 7 ... ♘e5.)

In short, 5 ♗e3, while logical, gives Black too much time.

The best attempt to punish Black for 4 ... ♗c5 is relatively unusual because it involves moving the a-pawn. This is 5 ♘b3! ♗b6 6 a4!. The White a-pawn threatens to go to a5 and push the Black Bishop off the board.

After 4 ... ♗c5 5 ♘b3 ♗b6 6 a4

At first glance, the cavalier attack by the a-pawn seems hopelessly naive. Novice players often try to activate their Rooks very early in the game by bringing them into play by means of a2-a4 and ♖a3 or h2-h4 and ♖h3. But their poor Rooks

usually get trapped on the third rank and come under a barrage of attacks by the enemy pieces. The novice learns to keep his Rooks on the first rank in the early stages of the game.

But here is a rare instance where a2-a4 makes some sense. If Black prevents a4-a5 by occupying a5 with his own pawn, he creates a slight hole at b5—that is, a square that has lost some of its pawn protection—because now ... a7-a6 can never be played.

A safer method is 6 ... a6. Then we get to see White's strategy in full. He will play 7 ♘c3 and then ♘d5 and ♗g5 after Black develops his King Knight. White would welcome an exchange of Knights on d5 because he could recapture with his e-pawn and—here's the point—follow up with ♖a3 or a4-a5 and ♖a4 with an advantage in space.

We speak of a spatial advantage when one side's pawns are farther advanced than the other side's and push the enemy pieces out of the way. White would have more space after, for example, 6 ... a6 7 ♘c3 ♕f6 (threatens mate on f2) 8 ♕e2 ♘ge7 9 ♘d5! ♘xd5 10 exd5 + ♘e7 11 a5 ♗a7 12 ♖a4 followed by ♖e4 or ♖f4.

Again, this is an unusual strategy in the opening but one that has several benefits, including the gain of time that results from ♘b3 and the advance of the a-pawn. It is worthwhile to test this position in friendly games to get a feel for White's position.

Black may also contest White's development with his queen.

b) **4 ... ♛f6.** We saw in the line beginning with 4 ... ♗c5 5 ♗e3 that 5 ... ♛f6 was a solid move. Is it a good move now? It is usually inadvisable to develop the Queen so early in the game, but here it has a useful point. Black's Queen will eventually go to g6, where it will exert pressure on White's Queenside and inhibit the development of White's King Bishop. For instance, 4 ... ♛f6 5 ♘b3 ♛g6 not only attacks White's e-pawn but also prevents White's Bishop from leaving the defense of the g-pawn.

But White has a better move than 5 ♘b3. Does 4 ... ♛f6 create a weakness for Black? If you are looking at the c7-square, you probably can see that 5 ♘b5! is a strong response. Black certainly doesn't want to defend c7 by abjectly retreating his Queen or by moving his King. He can defend it by playing ... ♗c5 and (after White defends f2) ... ♗b6. But after White plays ♗e3 Black's problems at c7 remain; e.g., 5 ... ♗c5 6 ♕e2 ♗b6 7 ♘1c3 ♘ge7 8 ♗e3.

c) **4 ... ♛h4.** This is the most daring effort to refute the Scotch Game. White's e-pawn becomes an immediate target and his pieces can become tangled in its defense, such as after 5 ♘c3 ♗b4! 6 ♕d3 ♘f6. But if White is willing to sacrifice the e-pawn, he can obtain a powerful attack. For example, 5 ♘b5 (pinpointing Black's c7 problem once

again) ♛xe4+ 6 ♗e2 and Black must play 6 ... ♔d8 to protect c7 because 6 ... ♛e5 loses control of c7 after 7 f4. The position after 6 ... ♔d8 7 0-0 a6 8 ♘1c3 ♛e8 9 ♘d4 offers White excellent chances because of his considerable lead in development and his prospects of exploiting the open e-file.

These ideas—4 ... ♗c5, 4 ... ♛f6, and 4 ... ♛h4—all contain elements of the strength of 4 ... ♘f6. But the Knight move, unlike the others, has no drawback. That is, it doesn't weaken any key square and it doesn't give up any important *option*. It is both aggressive and flexible.

5   ♘c3

How important it is to retain options will be revealed shortly, because Black can now play 5 ... ♗b4. If he had already committed his Bishop to c5, he would be understandably reluctant to spend more valuable time to move it again. But after 5 ♘c3 ♗b4 Black can enjoy his slight initiative a little longer, for the e-pawn is attacked again (now that

White's Knight on c3 is pinned by the Bishop).

Because of this slight initiative for Black, White has reason to look for other fifth moves. Instead of defending his e-pawn quietly, can he do it aggressively?

Clearly 5 e5? won't do because of 5 ... ♘xe5. But White can play 5 ♘xc6 first and then 6 e5. Since both moves are forcing—one is a capture, the other a threat to capture—they must be respected by Black.

Moreover, if Black plays 5 ... bxc6 (to avoid the exchange of Queens that may follow 5 ... dxc6) he will be faced with an unhappy choice of places to move his Knight after 6 e5. On e4 it will be unprotected, which will allow White to save time by attacking it with developing moves; e.g., 7 ♕f3! ♘c5 8 ♗c4 or 7 ... ♘g5 8 ♕g3. If the Knight goes to d5 it is also subject to further attack; e.g., 7 ♗d3 d6 8 exd6 cxd6 9 0-0 and 10 ♗e4!.

For Black to survive after 6 e5 he must play 6 ... ♕e7!. This is an unlikely move, the kind Black should be quite reluctant to make. On e7 the Queen blocks the development of the King Bishop and thereby delays Kingside castling for several moves. But after 6 ... ♕e7! White's e-pawn is under heavy pressure (7 ♗f4 d6 8 ♕e2 ♘d5 or 7 f4 d6). White can justify his daring sixth move only with 7 ♕e2, which has the same uncomfortable effect on White's development that 6 ... ♕e7 has on Black's. Also, 7 ♕e2 permits 7 ...

♘d5 with good play for Black because the Knight on d5 cannot be easily dislodged without serious consequences for White; e.g., 8 c4 ♗a6 (pinning the c-pawn) 9 f4? ♕b4 + and now 10 ♘c3 ♘xc3, or 10 ♗d2 ♕xb2, or 10 ♘d2 ♘xf4, and Black wins material.

After 5 ♘xc6 bxc6 6 e5 ♕e7 7 ♕e2 ♘d5 8 c4 ♗a6

White can improve on this line, but Black has an adequate game because he can challenge the White center with ... d7-d6 or ... f7-f6 and can complicate White's development with such moves as ... ♕b4 + , ... ♘f4, and ... ♘b4. And, although it is unusual in 1 e4 e5 openings, Black can safely castle on the Queenside in this particular variation as long as he has his Queen Bishop as a defensive piece.

Whereas the subvariation beginning with 5 ♘xc6 is aggressive, it is also double-edged. The safer and sounder way for White to continue is 5 ♘c3 despite ...

5 ...   ♗b4!

This is a forcing move that threatens 6 ... ♗xc3+ 7 bxc3 ♘xe4 or simply 6 ... ♘xe4. Black can also force matters with **5 ... ♗c5!?**. This is slightly different from the 4 ... ♗c5 we considered a few pages ago; that move could be met by 5 ♘b3 (5 ... ♗b4+ 6 c3!) whereas 6 ♘b3 in the present position is met by 6 ... ♗b4, pinning the White Knight on c3. Thus 6 ♘b3 accomplishes nothing.

However, **6 ♗e3** is a good response to 5 ... ♗c5 because 6 ... ♕f6—as in that previous line we mentioned—is now impossible. Black has to meet the threat of 7 ♘xc6 and 8 ♗xc5 in some other manner, such as 6 ... ♗b6. But when Black has committed his King Knight to f6, his Bishop is not so well placed on b6 because with the dark-square Bishop absent from the Kingside White has the nasty pin ♗g5 at the right moment. For example, 7 ♗e2 0-0 8 0-0 d6 and now 9 ♘xc6 followed by 10 ♗g5 sets up a pin that Black can't easily remove without

seriously weakening his King's position; e.g., 10 ... ♕d7 11 ♗xf6 or 10 ... h6 11 ♗h4 g5.

The most forceful alternative to 5 ... ♗b4 is **5 ... ♘xe4!?**. This capture is possible because 6 ♘xe4 ♕e7 regains the piece (7 ♗d3 ♘xd4; 7 ♕d3 d5). But this is one more example of unwarranted pawn-grabbing by a player with an under-developed position. Black simply doesn't have enough pieces in play to justify such a risky capture. White should play 6 ♘xe4 ♕e7 7 f3 d5 8 ♗b5!, which leads to his advantage after 8 ... ♗d7 9 0-0 dxe4 10 ♗xc6 bxc6 11 ♖e1 or 11 fxe4. Though Black's pawns on the Queenside are crippled, that's where he will probably have to castle because it will take too long to get castled on the Kingside.

6 ♘xc6

The pressure on White's e-pawn has become too great. He can create a pin of his own with 6 ♗g5, but it will be broken by 6 ... h6 (7 ♗xf6 ♕xf6 favors Black because he will be left with two excellent Bishops, and since Black hasn't castled yet, the advance of his Kingside pawns is not unduly risky). The moves 6 ♕d3 and 6 f3 are too clumsy or weakening to be good. White has better squares than d3 for his Queen and should not put it in the way of his King Bishop. And 6 f3 d5! exposes White's center to a stronger attack than the one after 7 ... d5 in the main line (see below), because here 7 exd5 would leave White with an ugly hole at e3 that could no longer be protected by a White pawn.

6 ... bxc6

7 ♗d3

What we said about 6 f3 also applies to positions that arise from 7 ♕d4 and 7 ♗d2. White's problems with his e-pawn continue after **7 ♕d4 ♕e7!** and his Queen will be an even bigger problem after 8 ♗d3 c5! 9 ♕c4 d5!. He can play 8 f3 instead of the Bishop move, but then 8 ... d5! adds decisive pressure to the e-pawn. Besides creating a weak e3-square, the move f2-f3 is risky because it opens the diagonal from b6 to the square usually reserved for White's castled King, g1. Black will eventually be able to seize that diagonal with ... ♗c5, and maybe he can do it while White's Queen is still sitting on d4.

Similarly, **7 ♗d2** lacks strength if White intends to prop up his pawn

center with 7 ... 0-0 8 ♗d3 d5 9 f3?. The weakening of the squares around White's King have planted the seeds of a combination: 9 ... ♗xc3 10 ♗xc3 dxe4 11 fxe4 ♘xe4! 12 ♗xe4 ♕h4+ and 13 ... ♕xe4.

But 7 ♗d3 makes sense. It develops the last Kingside piece, so White is now ready to castle. And it gives his Bishop a good diagonal (d3-h7) regardless of what happens in the center. By comparison, on c4 the Bishop would be under the constant threat that Black might play ... d5!, driving it away.

7 ... d5

It is largely a matter of taste rather than theory whether Black plays this now or a move or two later. If he prefers to play 7 ... 0-0 first he can move his d-pawn on the eighth move (not fearing 8 e5? ♖e8 9 ♕e2 d6). However, the immediate 7 ... d5 creates more *options;* for instance, a Black Queen check on e7 after 8 exd5.

We'll get to that in a moment; now it is important to consider what happens if Black doesn't play ... d5 at all.

That would ultimately mean ... d7-d6 instead, since the only convenient way to activate his undeveloped Bishop is by pushing the d-pawn one or two squares. Black can delay ... d7-d6 or ... d7-d5 for a while, but not indefinitely. For example, after **7 ... 0-0 8 0-0** he faces the prospect of 9 e5, which would drive his Knight from its excellent post on f6. The natural way of continuing would be 8 ... d6 or 8 ... ♖e8, but then 9 ♗g5! would have a cramping effect on Black's game.

The pinning ♗g5 move is White's major trump in the coming middlegame regardless of what Black does with his d-pawn. Once Black has castled he cannot get out of the pin without pain; e.g., after 8 ... ♖e8 9 ♗g5 h6 10 ♗h4 g5?! 11 ♗g3 d6 12 e5! dxe5 13 ♗xe5 White's pieces are superbly centralized and he is ready to exploit Black's many pawn weaknesses with ♕f3 (13 ... ♖xe5?? 14 ♗xh7+ and 15 ♕xd8).

Even if Black avoids weakening his Kingside with ... g5, he faces problems near his King. After 8 ... ♖e8 9 ♗g5 h6 10 ♗h4 d6 11 f4! ♗d7 (or 11 ... ♗b7) White continues with ♕f3 followed by ♖ael with the powerful threat of e4-e5 in the offing. Black's problems in this kind of middlegame include the lack of a good square for his Queen. And until the Queen moves, the Rooks remain unconnected and uncoordinated.

Earlier in this chapter we discussed the significance of bad pawns. Here it is important to consider what happens if Black musses up White's pawns by playing ... ♗xc3 at some point.

He can do it right now (7 ... ♗xc3+) and then make his choice between ... d7-d5 and ... d7-d6. But Black needs that Bishop a lot more than he needs the White pawns weak-

ened. If Black plays 7 ... ♗xc3+ 8 bxc3 d5?, White will exchange pawns on d5 and post his unchallenged Bishop—unchallenged because Black has just traded away his own dark-square Bishop—at a3, where it prevents Black from castling. Even if Black castles before playing ... d7-d5, White will gain more from ♗a3 in the middlegame than Black could hope to achieve from White's weak c-pawns in the endgame.

If after ... ♗xc3 Black plays the superior ... d7-d6 (instead of ... d7-d5), he limits the scope of White's Bishop on the a3-f8 diagonal. But he still has to worry about White's ♗g5!. The pin would once again give White the advantage because Black could not break it without weakening his own Kingside pawns. The Kingside pawns will count more heavily in the middlegame than White's c-pawns.

8 exd5!

It is tempting to play **8 e5** here, if only because it would be White's first really aggressive move since 3 d4. Black cannot answer 8 e5 effectively with 8 ... ♕e7—as he often can when e4-e5 is played earlier—because of 9 0-0! (9 ... ♕xe5?? 10 ♖e1 winning the Queen).

So the Knight must move from f6 after 8 e5. But to where? On d7 it would attack White's e-pawn again but would interfere with Black's pieces a bit. On e4 it would add pressure to White's c3-square, but that would lead to a liquidation of minor pieces and a drawish endgame; e.g., 8 ... ♘e4 9 ♗xe4 ♗xc3+ 10 bxc3 dxe4, with a symmetrical position. Each side would be left with a Bishop, but the two Bishops are on opposite-color squares, which limits either side's winning chances in the endgame.

Thus, Black's best bet is 8 ... ♘g4!. White can defend his e-pawn with a Bishop, a pawn, or a trap. The trap is only a momentary defense (9 0-0 ♘xe5?? 10 ♖e1 and if 10 ... ♕e7 11 f4) and would have to be followed up eventually by the Bishop move (♗f4) or the pawn move (f2-f4).

The chief defect of the defense 9 f4 is the weakness it creates on the diagonal leading from b6 to g1. For example, 9 f4 0-0 10 0-0? loses to 10 ... ♗c5+ 11 ♔h1 ♕h4! 12 h3 ♕g3 13 hxg4 ♕h4 mate!

The Bishop move is an improvement, but Black has the better of the game after 9 ♗f4 f6! (or 9 ... 0-0 and 10 ... f6) because White will have to exchange his e-pawn for Black's f-pawn under circumstances that favor Black's attacking chances along the f-file.

8 ...   cxd5

Another of those options offered by 7 ... d5 (and not by 7 ... 0-0 and 8 ... d5) is the clever interpolation of 8 ... ♕e7+. This check is annoying to the player who fully expects to checkmate Black in a vigorous Scotch middlegame. That's because, of the half a dozen different ways White may respond to the check, the only good response is to offer to exchange Queens (9 ♕e2)—hardly what White wants in a go-for-mate middlegame!

After 8 ... ♕e7+ White should not give up the option of castling by making a King move, and he doesn't want to walk into a bad pin with 9 ♗e3 ♘xd5!, which threatens to win material. Another alternative to 9 ♕e2 is to stick the Bishop on e2, but that is extremely passive and leaves White's pieces less actively posted than Black's after 9 ... cxd5 10 0-0 ♗b7.

Not long ago it was believed that 8 ... ♕e7+ 9 ♕e2 ♕xe2+ 10 ♔xe2 was dead even and likely to lead to a draw. True, the Queens have been removed and this tends to lessen the significance of any Kingside threats that may crop up for White in the normal Scotch lines. (It also virtually eliminates that powerful ♗g5 pin that White so often uses to constrict Black's pieces.)

But Black's problems remain after 10 ♔xe2 because his c- and d-pawns can be attacked before he completes his development. For example, 10 ... cxd5 11 ♘b5!, threatening ♘xc7+, is an annoying move, and it will be followed by ♗f4 and ♖d1 to add pressure against the target pawns. Black can interpolate 10 ... ♗xc3+ 11 bxc3 before recapturing on d5, but then White plays 12 ♗a3! with excellent play for his Bishops and the prospect of opening the game for his Rooks with c3-c4. Black can be mated in such an endgame just as he can in the middlegame.

Black can improve a bit in these lines by playing 9 ... cxd5 instead of 9 ... ♕xe2+ so that White will be the one to actually trade Queens with 10 ♕xe7+. But Black still has problems with his pawns; e.g., 10 ... ♔xe7 11 0-0 ♖d8 12 ♘b5! c6 13 ♘d4 and 14 ♗f4.

9	0-0	0-0
10	♗g5!	

This difficult position shows the trade-offs typical of a vigorously contested opening. White's pieces have more freedom and are likely to make more specific threats, especially against the King, for the next dozen moves or so.

But on the other side of the trade-off is Black's center. We began this chapter by showing how a typical pawn structure dominated by a White pawn at e4 favors the first player. Now it is Black who has more pawns in the center (a result, you will note, of his capturing toward the center with 6 ... bxc6 rather than away from it with 6 ... dxc6). The Black d-pawn serves to deny White the use of the squares c4 and e4. But because White's pieces are so well placed, Black will not be able to make good use of those squares either.

What happens now? Well, White begins with a threat: 11 ♗xf6 ♕xf6 12 ♘xd5 (12 ... ♕xb2? 13 ♖b1 winning a piece), or if 11 ... gxf6 12 ♘xd5! (12 ... ♕xd5?? 13 ♗xh7+ and 14 ♕xd5). This indicates a major theme of the middlegame: the attack on Black's central pawn, using the Bishop on g5, the Knight, and the Queen. After Black defends against the immediate threat, White can shift his Queen to f3 where it keeps up the pressure against the d-pawn, increases the pressure on f6, and prepares to take part in a Kingside attack. White will then have two Bishops and a Queen aimed at the enemy Kingside, and the Knight will soon be added. The best routes for the Knight are ♘e2-g3-f5 (or -h5) and ♘d1-e3-f5. The coordinated attack by a Knight on f5, a Bishop on g5, and a Queen on f3 would be nearly fatal for Black.

But Black also has something to say about this middlegame. He can play the position solidly with ... c7-c6, after which his center is secure, and he can get out of the pin on his Knight with ... ♕d6. Black's Bishops will have to find better squares than they have in the diagram, but the Queen Bishop will stand well on e6—and even better on g6, if it can get there (by way of ... ♗g4-h5-g6). The other Bishop can retreat to e7 to eliminate the problem of the pin, or to c5 for an attack on f2. Black can even scare up a Kingside attack of his own with ... ♕d6 and ... ♗a5-c7, threatening ... ♕xh2 mate.

Black can play aggressively with his central pawns rather than conservatively. He can start by safeguarding his d-pawn with 10 ... ♗e6 and ... ♗e7 so that his c-pawn can go to c5 in one move instead of two. Then he can prepare to push White's pieces back with ... c7-c5-c4 and ... d5-d4. In a later stage of the middlegame, he may even be able to create a passed d-pawn with ... d4-d3.

The result is a well-balanced struggle with plenty of room for enterprise by White or Black. The diagrammed position does not appear often in grandmaster games nowadays, but this is not a reflection on the Scotch Game. White may have better winning chances (or fewer losing chances) in other openings and so the Scotch is not seen in the most prestigious events as often today as it was at the turn of the century.

Instructive Game No. 1

White: Miyasaka
Black: Tarazi

World Team Championship
Siegen 1970

1	e4	e5
2	♘f3	♘c6
3	d4	exd4
4	♘xd4	♘f6

As we've emphasized earlier, if Black can play ... d7-d5 safely in the early stages of the Scotch Game, he can undermine White's pawn in the center. Usually this is enough to neutralize White's slight central superiority and balance the chances. An obvious question, then, is: Why not ... d7-d5 at the earliest possible moment, the fourth move?

The answer is that Black does not have enough pieces developed to avoid a tactical refutation. This is not unusual. Often at an early stage of the game a move can be justified by a sound positional plan but still be very wrong for tactical reasons. Here the refutation of 4 ... d5 is 5 ♘xc6 bxc6 6 exd5 cxd5 7 ♗b5 + !, since Black's natural reaction to the check (7 ... ♗d7) blocks the protection of his d-pawn (8 ♕xd5). Of course, Black can play 6 ... ♕xd5 instead of

6 ... cxd5?, but then 7 ♕e2+ followed by ♘c3 gives White a lead in development and the possibility of attacking Black's weakened c-pawns.

5	♘c3	♗b4!
6	♘xc6	bxc6
7	♗d3	d5
8	exd5	cxd5
9	0-0	0-0
10	♗g5!	

If White passes up the opportunity to impose this pin, he will have little to show for his work in the opening and may have to struggle to avoid disadvantage. For example, 10 ♘e2, though logical, lacks any immediate bite, and Black can play 10 ... ♖e8 11 c3 ♗d6 followed by ... ♖b8. Black will then have control of the open e-file and the half-open (that is, open only from Black's side) b-file. He will be able to occupy the e4-square with his Knight and attack the Kingside with ... ♕h4 and ... ♗g4. In short, he will have a fine game.

10	...	c6
11	♕f3!	♗e7

If Black is willing to go into an endgame, his last move is unnecessary. For example, he can try 11 ... ♖e8 and meet 12 ♗xf6 with 12 ... ♕xf6 13 ♕xf6 gxf6. Black's Kingside pawns are not pretty, but as compensation he has very active play in the endgame. He can put a Rook on b8 and exert pressure on b2 with ... ♗d6-e5!, for instance. When White puts a Rook on the e-file, Black can answer with ... ♖e6 or ... ♖e5, for if White exchange Rooks Black's pawns get straightened out.

The key point here is *endgame*. After 11 ... ♖e8 12 ♗xf6 Black wouldn't dare play 12 ... gxf6? because his Kingside would be very vulnerable with the Queens on the board (e.g., immediately 13 ♕h5 threatening 14 ♕xh7+). By playing 11 ... ♗e7 Black keeps the option of staying in the middlegame (by recapturing on f6 with the Bishop) and clears the b-file for pressure by his Rook at b8.

12 ♖ae1

Now is the time for White to use the open file, and the only question is which Rook to put on e1. White chooses the Queen Rook so that he can use the other Rook in support of f4-f5 in case Black plays ... ♗e6. The difference between ♖ae1 and ♖fe1 is minor, since White is likely to play ♖e2 and ♖1e1 regardless of which Rook is moved first.

12	...	h6!

This might be a very bad move later, but now it's good. Delaying this move permits White to build up a terrific attack against g7 and h6 by means of ♘d1-e3-f5, and then even a slight weakening of the Kingside pawns could be fatal. But Black has not yet committed himself to any particular form of counterplay, and this move is useful because it forces White to make a decision. 13 ♗h4 permits 13 ... ♖b8 (attacking the b-pawn) followed by 14 ... ♖b4!. This development of the Rook is somewhat irregular, but quite effective since the Bishop on h4 will be driven back to the less useful g3-square.

13 ♗xh6!?

This is brilliant—but not good enough because with best play Black has a safe draw. In fact, White has as much chance of losing after this sacrifice as Black. White can win two pawns for the piece, but if Black defends accurately he will be forced to end the game with a draw by perpetual check. For this reason, 13 ♗c1! and ♘d1-e3-f5 is a better course for White.

| 13 | ... | gxh6 |
| 14 | ♕e3 | |

This is White's idea: he attacks the Bishop at e7 and also the pawn at h6. If the Queen gets to h6, White can threaten mate by bringing a Rook to the g-file or by eliminating the Black

Knight at f6 (which defends against ♕h7 mate). The play now becomes very difficult.

| 14 | ... | ♖e8? |

This is logical. It defends the Bishop and prepares to cover the Kingside with another piece (... ♗f8-g7). But it is inferior to the more forceful 14 ... d4!. Then White would have to play 15 ♕xh6 because 15 ♕xe7 ♕xe7 16 ♖xe7 dxc3 would leave him a piece behind in the endgame. But after 15 ♕xh6 ♕d6! White could not bring a Rook to the g-file via e5 or e3.

He could, however, force a draw by checking repeatedly at h6 and g5. If he tried to reserve that possibility for later, as a last-ditch resource to bail out of a lost position, then after 16 ♕g5+ ♔h8 17 ♖xe7!? ♕xe7 18 ♘e4?, for example, the chances would turn in Black's favor after 18 ... ♘g8!, since there would no longer be a perpetual check.

15 ♕xh6

Black is in serious trouble now because of White's threat to bring a Rook to the g-file. Black cannot move his Knight: if 15 ... ♘g4? 16 ♕h7+ and 17 ♕h8 mate, or if 15 ... ♘e4 16 ♘xe4 dxe4 17 ♗xe4 and a big check on h7 next move. He would like to play 15 ... ♗f8, but after 16 ♖xe8, either f6 or h7 will be unprotected when Black recaptures. Finally, 15 ... ♕d6 is too late (16 ♖e3! and 17 ♖g3+), and so is 15 ... d4 (16 ♖e5!).

| 15 | ... | ♕c7 |
| 16 | ♖e3 | ♗g4 |

This is the only way to block the g-file and stave off immediate mate—except for sacrificing the Queen when White plays ♖g3+.

| 17 | h3! | d4 |
| 18 | ♖g3! | |

Black may have thought he was surviving, but now he realizes that White's real threat is not 19 hxg4 but rather 19 ♖xg4+! ♘xg4 20 ♕h7+ ♔f8 21 ♕h8 mate. Even if Black's King is given an escape from f8 to avoid this mate, there's another mate available to White: 18 ... ♗d8, for instance, clears the e7-square, but it allows 19 ♖xg4+ ♘xg4 20 ♕h7+ ♔f8 21 ♕h8+ ♔e7 22 ♖e1+ ♔d6 23 ♕xd4 mate. Now Black makes a valiant attempt to protect the h8-square.

| 18 | ... | ♕e5 |

| 19 | f4! | ♕e6 |
| 20 | ♖xg4+ | |

Now Black must give up his Queen because 20 ... ♘xg4 loses, as before, to 21 ♕h7+ and 22 ♕h8 mate. The game ended with: **20 ... ♕xg4 21 hxg4 dxc3 22 g5! ♗c5+ 23 ♔h1 ♘g4 24 ♕h7+ ♔f8 25 ♗c4! ♔e7** (25 ... ♖e7 occupies the flight square Black needs to avoid ♕h8 mate) **26 ♕xf7+ ♔d6 27 ♖d1+ ♗d4 28 ♖xd4+ ♔c5 29 ♗e2! ♔xd4 30 ♕c4+ ♔e3 31 ♗xg4 ♔f2 32 ♕xc3 ♖h8+ 33 ♗h3** (were it not for this Bishop, Black would have mated White with just his King and Rook!) **33 ... ♖ae8 34 ♔h2 ♖h7 35 ♕g3+, Black resigns** (White's next moves would have been 36 ♕d3+ and 37 ♕xh7).

Instructive Game No. 2

White: A Nimzovich
Black: A. Rubinstein

Vilna 1912

1	e4	e5
2	♘f3	♘c6
3	d4	exd4
4	♘xd4	♘f6
5	♘c3	♗b4

Black can also prepare to develop his Bishop at g7 with 5 ... g6 (or a move earlier with 4 ... g6). The type of position to which that leads is not as aggressive for Black as the one in the main line, for there is less immediate pressure on White's e-pawn and White does not have to play ♘xc6 right away. For example, 5 ... g6 6 ♗e3 ♗g7 and now 7 ♘xc6 bxc6 8 e5! is good for White because 8 ... ♘d5 loses a pawn after 9 ♘xd5, and 8 ... ♕e7 just loses a piece. Instead, Black has to retreat the Knight to g8 (8 ... ♘h5? 9 g4 traps the piece) and admit he has lost time; e.g., 8 ... ♘g8 9 ♗d4 followed by ♕d2 and 0-0-0.

| 6 | ♘xc6 | bxc6 |
| 7 | ♗d3 | |

In contrast to the note above, 7 e5 now runs into 7 ... ♕e7 or 7 ... ♘d5.

7	...	0-0
8	0-0	d5
9	exd5	cxd5
10	♗g5	c6
11	♘e2	

The maneuver of this Knight to d4 has some good thinking behind it. But it is too slow—that is, it makes no immediate threats and eases some of the pressure on Black. That extra freedom allows Black to get out of the pin on his Knight and to take over the initiative by making threats of his own.

| 11 | ... | ♖e8! |

Black should not hurry to weaken his pawns with 11 ... c5. Although that move keeps White's Knight out of d4, it also removes the protection of the d-pawn that Black established

with 10 ... c6. White can meet 11 ... c5 with 12 c3! ♗a5 (note that now the Bishop cannot retreat to d6 or e7) 13 ♘f4, threatening both 14 ♘h5 followed by capturing on f6 to disrupt Black's Kingside pawns, and 14 ♗xf6 ♕xf6 15 ♘xd5 winning a pawn.

| 12 | ♘d4 | ♕d6 |

Black gets out of the pin, making possible his next move, ... ♘e4. On e4 the Knight surveys several important squares and threatens the Bishop on g5. After 13 ♕f3 ♘e4 14 ♗e3, for example, Black gains time with 14 ... ♕g6, threatening to win the Queen with 15 ... ♗g4 16 ♕g3 ♗d6. By means of these little harassing threats, Black would find excellent squares for his Bishops and would take control of the e- and b-files with his Rooks before White could get organized.

| 13 | ♗h4? | ♘e4! |

Black has an excellent position: his Queen and one of his Rooks are already developed and his minor pieces compare favorably with White's.

♛f3, the move White should have played earlier, now walks into 14 ... ♞d2!, winning the Exchange.

14	c3	♝c5
15	f3	

White has an uncomfortable game because Black's Knight, backed up by his strong center, denies his Queen and Bishops their best squares. If White gives up a Bishop for the Knight (15 ♝xe4 or 15 ♝g3), Black's two good Bishops, combined with his control of the e-file after ... ♜e7 and ... ♜ae8, would keep his advantage alive for many moves.

15	...	♛h6!

This is much better than any Knight retreat. Now White must keep his dark-square Bishop on the board because his last move (15 f3) weakened the dark squares around his King—especially e3 and f2.

16	fxe4?	♛xh4
17	exd5	cxd5

Black can even win a pawn here with 17 ... ♝xd4+ 18 cxd4 ♛xd4+ 19 ♚h1 ♛xd5. That would ease White's game, however, by eliminating Black's obnoxious Bishop and letting White make his first threats with 20 ♛c2! (coming up: ♝xh7+ or ♝c4). Black correctly

keeps his Bishop so that he can attack the Kingside with ... ♝d6.

18	♝f5	g6!
19	♝xc8	♜axc8
20	♜f2	♜e4!

The Black Knight that was exchanged off four moves ago has been replaced by an equally useful Rook. Black keeps up the pressure on d4 and prepares to take unchallengeable control of the board's only open file.

21	g3	♛e7

Black must decide how best to use his advantage. He can play "brilliantly" with 21 ... ♜xd4!, which would give him the advantage in the endgame following 22 gxh4 ♜xd1+ 23 ♜xd1 ♝xf2+, or 22 cxd4 ♛xd4. But he also has chances of winning in the middlegame, and he decides to keep the Queens on the board.

22	♛d2	f5
23	♜d1	♜e3

71

Black uses his control of the e-file to take more and more squares away from White's pieces. White can't move his Knight because of the dangerous diagonal leading to his King (24 ♘c2?? ♖e2! 25 ♕xe2 ♕xe2), and he has very few places for his Queen and Rooks.

24	♔g2	♕e4+
25	♔g1	

This clearly demonstrates White's helplessness. He would like to keep his King off the diagonal of Black's Bishop, but 25 ♘f3 would create danger on another diagonal because of 25 ... ♖d8 (to stop 26 ♕xd5+) and ... g6-g5-g4!

25	...	♗b6
26	♖f4	♕e7
27	♔g2	♖c4!

Black's d-pawn gives him two outposts, c4 and e4, and he is making good use of both of them. Now he threatens 28 ... ♗xd4 and 29 ... ♖e2+. Since the Knight cannot move because of ... ♖e2+, and since the King has no good moves (28 ♔f2 ♖e4!), White tries to solve all his positional problems with one tactical flash.

28	♘xf5?!	

Now 28 ... gxf5? 29 ♕xd5+ ♕e6 30 ♕xe6+ and 31 ♖xc4 wins for White.

28	...	♖e2+
29	♔h3	♕e6!

White loses the Knight in exchange for only a pawn or two—and that's not enough. The endgame after 30 ♕xd5 ♕xd5 31 ♖xd5 ♖xf4 32 gxf4 gxf5 33 ♖xf5 ♖xb2 34 a4 ♖b3 would be hopeless. Black won in a few more moves.

Part Six
Petroff Defense

William Hartston

White	Black
1 e4	e5
2 ♘f3	♘f6

This is the move which characterizes Petroff's Defense. White's second move attacked the Black pawn on e5, and Black retaliates by threatening the White e-pawn. The spirit of this defense is obvious right at the start: it is counterattack!

3 ♘xe5

White accepts the invitation to capture Black's undefended pawn. He can also try to open the position with **3 d4,** hoping to embarrass the Black Knight after 4 ... exd4 4 e5. However, after 4 ... ♘e4 5 ♕xd4

d5 6 exd6 ♘xd6 Black comes out of it with an equal game. He is set to regain lost time by attacking the White Queen with ... ♘c6.

Note how all four center pawns are quickly exchanged in this line. The immediate reduction in tension is quite characteristic of the Petroff. White is hard put to demonstrate any advantage after such early exchanges. The move **3 ♗c4,** inviting Black into a Giuoco Piano or Two Knights Defense after 3 ... ♘c6, is a riskier attempt by White to get some advantage. The risk is that Black will decline the invitation and instead take the undefended pawn with 3 ... ♘xe4. Then 4 ♘xe5 d5 would only lose time for White, so he would have to make a full commitment to the attacking spirit: with the pawn sacrifice 4 ♘c3 ♘xc3 5 dxc3, the open lines might provide a sufficient attack to compensate for the pawn.

3 ...   d6!

Black must take care before reclaiming his pawn. The immediate **3 ... ♘xe4?** is a bad mistake due to the reply 4 ♕e2! Any move of the

Black Knight from e4 would then allow the devastating discovered check 5 ♘c6 + !, winning the Black Queen. Supporting the Knight with 4 ... d5 only delays the disaster (5 d3). This is a typical consequence of careless play by Black in the Petroff. This opening is by its nature liable to lead to the quick disappearance of both e-pawns. Black must take care to avoid accidents on the open e-file that results.

In fact, after 3 ... ♘xe4? 4 ♕e2 Black can restrict his losses by replying 4 ... ♕e7 5 ♕xe4 d6 6 d4 dxe5. But although losing "only" a pawn is not the disaster that losing the Queen is, giving away a pawn in the opening must be avoided. By playing 3 ... d6, Black forces the White Knight to retreat, after which, as we shall see, the pawn on e4 can safely be captured.

4   ♘f3

The most natural square for the Knight's retreat. Instead, 4 ♘c4 ♘xe4 leaves the White Knight somewhat out on a limb and vulnerable to later attack by the advance of the Black d-pawn.

4   ...   ♘xe4

Finally the pawn can be safely taken.

5   d4

White no longer has anything to gain by pinning the Knight with 5 ♕e2. Black simply replies 5 ... ♕e7, when 6 d3 ♘f6 leads only to the exchange of Queens on the open e-file. Although the Petroff Defense is motivated by the desire to counterattack, the open line in variations like this can easily bring about exchanges. This is why many Petroff variations have a drawish tendency. Only when White tries for a real opening advantage can we expect a truly cut-and-thrust battle.

By playing 5 d4, White opens the diagonal for his Queen Bishop while staking a claim for central space. Instead, bringing out another piece with 5 ♘c3 only encourages Black to exchange with 5 ... ♘xc3 6 dxc3 ♗e7. Black will then castle on the Kingside with a perfectly satisfactory position, free of weaknesses.

A more ambitious idea is 5 c4. This curious pawn move is based on the idea of following up with 6 d4, after which the two White pawns on c4 and d4 will guarantee him more space for the middlegame. The idea of playing c2-c4 first is to dissuade Black from playing ... d7-d5. Nevertheless, after 5 c4 ♗e7 6 d4 0-0 7 ♗d3 ♘f6 Black finishes his development in peace and can continue happily with ... ♗g4 and ... ♘c6 with no worries for the middlegame.

5 ...   d5

By moving his d-pawn for the second time, Black supports the Knight on e4 while also allowing his Bishop to be developed at the active square d6. The alternative 5 ... ♗e7 6 ♗d3 ♘f6 is more passive, but playable. The main question in this position revolves about the Knight on e4. If Black meekly retreats it, he will find himself slightly behind in development and fighting only for equality. By trying to maintain it at its aggressive post, he continues in the bold spirit which motivated his second move. Note that after 5 ... d5, Black appears to have gained a move since his Knight is on e4 compared with the White one on f3. Therefore, White must try to prove that Black's Knight has taken its challenging step prematurely.

6 ♗d3

The first stage in White's plan to

get rid of Black's Knight on e4. His plan is to attack the Knight itself with such moves as ♘bd2 (or ♘c3), ♖e1 (after castling), and ♕c2 (after moving the c-pawn), while combining these direct operations with plans to undermine the pawn at d5 which gives the Knight its support. Any retreat or exchange of the Black Knight on e4 will be to White's advantage since it will tend to accentuate his lead in development.

6 ...   ♗d6

This is the move most consistent with Black's aggressive outlook. He envisages a development scheme with ... 0-0, ... ♗g4, and ... f7-f5, aiming for an attack against the White castled King. The slight drawback of this move is that it cuts off the Queen's defense of the d5 pawn, thus making that pawn more vulnerable to White's undermining operations. Besides 6 ... ♗d6, Black has a number of other possibilities:

a) **6 ... &f5** has the idea of adding support to the Knight, but after 7 0-0 &e7 8 &e1 0-0 9 c4 c6 10 &b3 Black begins to feel the absence of the Bishop from his Queenside. The idea of bringing the White Queen to b3 with simultaneous attack on the d- and b-pawns is a common theme when Black develops his Queen Bishop early in the game.

b) **6 ... &g4** is another aggressive Bishop move. White's simplest reply is 7 &e2, adding to his attack on the Knight and forcing 7 ... &e7, after which Black finds that his Kingside development is gummed up.

c) **6 ... &c6** is a try for quick Queenside development. After 7 0-0 White already threatens unpleasant pressure on the open file with 8 &e1 so Black is obliged to block the line with 7 ... &e7 (see the next paragraph).

d) **6 ... &e7** 7 0-0 &c6 reaches the same position as in the above line with 6 ... &c6. Black's Bishop is less actively placed on e7 than on d6, but it blocks the open e-file and allows the Queen to maintain its protection of the d-pawn, and these two factors make it hard for White to gain any advantage. White's best plan is still to play &e1 followed by c2-c4 and to continue trying to undermine the support of the Knight on e4.

e) **6 ... &d6** is also sometimes played here. On d6 the Knight keeps an eye on the c4-square,

which makes it more difficult for White to play c2-c4. Nevertheless, retreating the Knight is not truly in the spirit of the opening. White can continue by advancing his own Knight after 7 0-0 &e7 8 &e5, to be followed by &f3 and &e1, with his men actively poised for an eventual attack on the Black King.

In general, Black does best to develop his Kingside as quickly as possible. The open e-file makes it important for him to castle quickly for the sake of King safety. For that reason, the most popular moves, as well as the most natural ones, have always been 6 ... &e7 and 6 ... &d6.

7 0-0

White brings his King to safety and prepares to put his Rook on the open file with 8 &e1. Instead, the immediate attack on Black's d-pawn with **7 c4** looks attractive, but it allows the surprising reply 7 ... &b4+!, taking advantage of the fact that White is still not castled. Although this is the second move by an already developed piece, the confusion it creates in White's camp is worth the lost time. After 8 &bd2 0-0 9 0-0 &xd2 10 &xd2 &g4, for example, Black develops easily and freely. White needs to be able to follow c2-c4 with &c3 if his pressure against d5 is going to mean anything. By forcing the Knight to develop at d2 instead of c3, Black's Bishop check fully justifies itself by taking the sting out of White's plan.

7 ...   0-0

The Black King scuttles to safety just in time. In view of the threat of ♖e1, putting pressure on the pinned Knight, Black has no sensible alternative.

8 c4!

This move has three important points: one, the attack on the d-pawn challenges the support of Black's Knight (8 ... dxc4?? would lose a piece to 9 ♗xe4); two, White frees the c2-square for his Queen so that it may be added to the attack on the e4-square; three, the diagonal from d1 to a4 is opened to allow the option of ♕b3, adding to the pressure on d5 and attacking b7.

Instead, **8 ♘c3** is an interesting alternative. By attacking the Knight at e4 and the pawn on d5, White forces his opponent to come to a

decision. However, after 8 ... ♘xc3 9 bxc3 ♗g4 Black has no difficulties. White can rid himself of the doubled pawns by playing 10 c4, but he has little prospect of advantage.

8 ...   ♘f6

Finally Black decides that he can support his advanced Knight no longer. Nevertheless, the retreat may be considered justified in that White has been tempted to advance his c-pawn. Now any exchange of White's c-pawn for Black's d-pawn will result in the isolation of the White d-pawn. This means that the pawn could later become a target for Black to work on since it could no longer be defended by another pawn.

In many ways, **8 ... c6** looks like Black's most natural reply, defending the attacked pawn. But it leaves Black with problems after 9 ♕c2!, because the threat of 10 ♗xe4 dxe4 11 ♕xe4, winning a pawn, is hard to meet. For instance, 9 ... ♗f5 lets White increase the attack on c4 with 10 ♘c3, since 10 ... ♘xc3 would be met by 11 ♗xf5!. Such variations are quite common in this line and illustrate the sort of problems Black can have in maintaining his Knight at e4. In retreating it, Black decides that discretion is the better part of valor.

9 ♘c3

It is tempting to gain time with **9 c5**, attacking the Bishop and forcing it to retreat to e7. This is not clearly advantageous for White, however. Advancing the pawn to c5 takes the pressure off the Black center and leaves the d5-pawn solidly supporting the Black position. Moreover, the pawn on c5 may itself be undermined later with ... b7-b6. Note that after 9 c5 ♗e7 White still has no more pieces developed than his opponent, and so he should not expect to be able to make good use of the space gained on the Queenside by the pawn advance.

9 ...   **dxc4**

Black resolves the central tension by exchanging pawns. Although he gives up his central pawn, he also isolates the White d-pawn, which has no pawn on either adjacent file to defend it and will therefore need constant defending by pieces. White hopes at least to compensate for this by getting attacking chances along the open e-file and the lines leading to the Black King. In such positions, White's pawn on d4 supports a Knight on e5 while Black, who has no pawn in the center, finds it hard to create good central outposts for his pieces.

10   **♗xc4**   **♗g4**

Black pins the Knight before it can reach e5. The pin, and the consequent threat to exchange the Knight, is also part of Black's plan of attacking the White d-pawn. Since the Knight is one of its defenders, any threat to this piece increases the vulnerability of the pawn.

The chances in this position are about equal. Black must take care not to be driven into passivity, since otherwise White's greater freedom of action may enable him to build up a strong attacking position. White too, while ensuring that his d-pawn is always adequately protected, must endeavor to maintain the initiative so that Black does not have time to organize an attack on the d-pawn.

Instructive Game No. 1

White: A. Karpov
Black: V. Korchnoi

Candidates Match, Moscow 1974
Game 6

1	e4	e5
2	♘f3	♘f6
3	♘xe5	d6
4	♘f3	♘xe4
5	d4	d5
6	♗d3	♗e7

Although 6 ... ♗d6 is the more overtly aggressive move, the more modest development can also be a part of attacking intentions by Black, as we shall see.

7	0-0	♘c6

With this move Black immediately initiates active play. His idea is to attack the pawn on d4 with this Knight and then increase the pressure by pinning the defending Knight with ... ♗g4. Castling is postponed, for with an extra move White could seize the initiative with ♖e1 or c2-c4.

8	♖e1	♗g4

An interesting position that clearly shows the ideas of both sides. White has systematically developed his pieces with a view to attacking the bold Knight on e4, and his last move threatened ♗xe4 to win a pawn.

Black replied by counterattacking the White d-pawn. Now White gains nothing by playing 9 ♗xe4 dxe4 10 ♖xe4 because of 10 ... ♗xf3, after which White must either give back the pawn with 11 ♕xf3 ♘xd4 or submit to the wreckage of his pawns and his King's safety with 11 gxf3. In this last case, the pawns on f3, f2, and h2 would be vulnerable, and the half-open g-file would add to White's defensive problems. Despite the pawn less, Black would have a clear advantage.

9	c3!

White defends his d-pawn. Now the threat of capturing twice on e4 must be taken seriously. Note that this modest pawn move also frees the way for White's Queen to emerge at b3.

9	...	f5!

Black must play consistently; he cannot afford to lose time by retreating the Knight. The pawn move further advertises Black's intention of taking an aggressive stance on the Kingside.

10 ♕b3!

White can now afford to allow 10 ... ♗xf3 11 gxf3. Then, when the Knight on e4 retreats, White captures the d-pawn or the b-pawn with his Queen. Black, his King still stuck in the middle, would have little chance of developing the initiative necessary to take advantage of the weaknesses on f3, f2, and h2.

10 ... 0-0!

The position is becoming very tense. Black calculates that he can allow 11 ♕xb7 since the reply 11 ... ♖f6 would threaten 12 ... ♗xf3 or 12 ... ♖b8. One possibility is 12 ♘e5? ♘xe5 13 dxe5 ♖b6 and White loses his Queen.

White does not win a pawn with 11 ♗xe4 fxe4 12 ♖xe4 because of 12 ... ♗xf3.

11 ♘bd2!

Another accurate move. White maintains his threats to the b7-pawn but, more important, he now exploits the pin on Black's d-pawn by his Queen. White threatens 12 ♘xe4 fxe4 13 ♗xe4 winning a pawn, since now that his Knight on f3 is protected by the other Knight, Black can't win back the pawn with ... ♗xf3.

Instead, 11 ♘fd2? might look

attractive, since it threatens to force the enemy pieces back with f2-f3, but this move allows the surprising sacrifice 11 ... ♘xf2! 12 ♔xf2 ♗h4+ 13 g3 f4!, and all the Black pieces combine in attacking the White King. This is a typical example of Black's attacking potential in this variation if White is just a little careless.

11 ... ♔h8

Black must move his King to escape the consequences of the pin on his d-pawn.

12 h3

Again, 12 ♕xb7 ♖f6 gives Black a promising attacking position. The threat would then be 13 ... ♖b8 driving the White Queen to a6, the only available square, after which Black would play 14 ... ♘xd4! uncovering an attack on the Queen by the Rook on f6. After 12 ♕xb7 ♖f6 13 ♕b3! Black plays 13 ... ♖g6, shifting the Rook to the same file as

White's King. With so many pieces then joining in the attack on the Kingside, Black would have a fine game for his pawn investment.

12 ... &h5?

Misjudging how long the b-pawn could safely be left undefended. 12 ... &xf3 13 ©xf3 ¤b8 is the safe course.

13 ©xb7! ¤f6
14 ©b3 ¤g6

With the Black Bishop still on g4 and the move h2-h3 omitted, this would threaten attacking gestures such as ... &h3. In the changed circumstances, the Black attack is considerably less potent. In view of this, the right move is 14 ... g5!, hoping to open lines by further advancing the g-pawn.

15 &e2!

A good defensive move which adds support to the Knight on f3 while also setting up the possibility of moving the Knight and attacking the Bishop on h5.

15 ... &h4
16 ¤f1

Defending against the threat of 16 ... &xf2+. Despite Black's aggressive formation, his attack lacks focus and White's defenses are completely adequate. For example,

16 ... ©g5 is calmly met by 17 ©xh4 ©xh3+ 18 ©h2 ©xh4 19 g3 and White's attack on the pieces on h3, h4, and h5 will win material.

16 ... &xf3
17 ©xf3 &xf2+

Although Black gets a Rook and a pawn for his Bishop and Knight, White will remain with a dominating position. Two minor pieces usually prove to be far more versatile than a Rook in the middlegame, and this is no exception.

18 ¤xf2 ©xf2
19 ©xf2 ©d6

Black hopes to play 20 ... ©g3+ with a big attack, but Karpov shows that White's defenses are still fully adequate.

20 ©g5!

Preventing the threatened check and also threatening 21 ©f7+, forking King and Queen.

20 ... ¤f8
21 ©a3! ©d8
22 &f4

The game is decided. Black's attack is over and White has a decisive material advantage.

22 ... h6
23 ©f3 ¤e8
24 &d3 ¤e4!?

Hoping for complications after 25 ♗xe4 fxe4 26 ♘e5 ♖f6. But White can ignore the Rook and avoid trouble.

25	g3!	♖f6
26	♕c5	g5

27 ♘xg5!

A dynamic way to put an end to the resistance. In an open position, such as the one that now results, the two Bishops radiate power across the board.

27	...	hxg5
28	♗xg5	♖ee6
29	♖e1	♕g8
30	h4	♖g6
31	♖xe6	

In this position Black lost by overstepping the time limit. After 31 ... ♖xe6 32 ♗xf5, White's two powerful Bishops and three extra pawns easily outclass the Black Rook and Knight.

Instructive Game No. 2

White: Norman-Hansen
Black: Andersen

Copenhagen 1934

1	e4	e5
2	♘f3	♘f6
3	♘xe5	d6
4	♘f3	♘xe4
5	d4	d5
6	♗d3	♗d6
7	0-0	0-0
8	c4	♗g4!?

Black boldly ignores the attack on his d-pawn, preferring quick development. The idea is not totally correct, but it demands accurate play by White if he is to defend successfully against the coming attack.

9 cxd5 f5!

Now we see the point of Black's idea. This pawn was slated to take over the defense of the Knight after the d-pawn was captured, but first the Bishop had to be developed so as not to be hemmed in by the pawn on f5.

10 ♘c3

10 ♖e1? is an instructive mistake, giving the opponent the chance for a nice sacrifice: 10 ... ♗xh2+! 11 ♔xh2 (11 ♘xh2 loses the Queen) 11 ... ♘xf2 12 ♕e2 (the Queen must protect the Bishop on d3) 12 ... ♘xd3 13 ♕xd3 ♗xf3, and if White recaptures on f3, Black has 14 ... ♕h4+! followed by taking the Rook on e1 and ending up with the net gain of the Exchange, or if White doesn't recapture on f3 Black ends up with an extra pawn or two.

10 ...   ♘d7!

Having surrendered one pawn, Black must be prepared to invest more if he is to keep the initiative.

11 h3!

As we shall see, this move is useful for the defense.

11	...	♗h5
12	♘xe4	fxe4
13	♗xe4	♘f6
14	♗f5!	

Note that this move would be unplayable if the Black Bishop were still on g4. Now Black cannot play 14 ... ♘xd5? due to 15 ♗e6+.

14 ...   ♕h8

Black is now two pawns behind but threatens to regain one with ♘xd5. He still hopes for attacking chances along the f-file. White's Knight on f3 is pinned, so White has only two reasonable choices: to grit his teeth and try to withstand the pressure or to play the double-edged g2-g4, which breaks the pin but also exposes his King to a potentially strong draft.

15 ♗e6?

White insists on hanging on to his d5 pawn, but the Bishop is badly placed here and cannot return to the defense. 15 g4! is the right move, after which Black should not have enough attack for his sacrificed pawn.

15 ...   ♘e4!

Black threatens to disrupt the pawns sheltering the White King with 16 ... ♗xf3. Now White has no real choice and must play g2-g4 anyway.

16	g4	♗g6
17	♔g2	♕f6
18	♗e3	♖ae8

Now all Black's pieces are actively involved in the attack. The dislocated position of the Bishop on e6 makes it hard for White to give enough support to the poor Knight on f3.

19 h4

White wants to play h4-h5 to drive away the troublesome Bishop, but Black does not intend to give him time.

19 ...   Bxe6!

Just a preliminary sacrifice. Watch what comes next!

20 dxe6   Nc3!

A fine clearance sacrifice. The sole point is to vacate the e4-square for the Bishop.

21 bxc3

White has no choice; his Queen is attacked, and 21 g5 would only encourage 21 ... Qxe6 and then the Black Queen enters on g4 with devastating effect. This explains why Black found it necessary to give up the Rook on e6 before jettisoning his Knight.

21 ...   Be4!

A short while ago the Knight on f3 was pinned on the d1-h5 diagonal. Now this same Bishop does an even better job in the other direction. The threat of ... Bxf3 + (or ... Qxf3 + if the White Queen runs away) cannot be satisfactorily met. Although White is, at the moment, a Rook and two pawns ahead, he is dead lost.

22 Kh3   Qxf3 + !

Now it is checkmate in six moves.

23 Qxf3   Rxf3 +
24 Kg2   Rg3 +

Double check! The King must move.

25 Kh2   Rg2 +
26 Kh1

After 26 Kh3 Black mates at once with 26 ... Rh2.

26 ...   Rh2 +
27 Kg1   Rh1 mate

An elegant finish. The White King was forced, rung, by rung, down the ladder to his doom.

Part Seven
King's Gambit Accepted
Edmar Mednis

White	Black
1 e4	e5
2 f4	

With his second move White offers the King's Gambit. A gambit is the sacrifice of a pawn or more in the opening, and what White is doing here is sacrificing a pawn on the Kingside; specifically, the f-pawn.

What does White hope to achieve? By tempting Black's e-pawn to move to f4, White hopes to lessen Black's influence in the center and to establish his own clear superiority there with an early d2-d4. Also, since White's f-pawn will disappear, he expects that his King Rook will find promising action along the f-file once the

Black pawn has been captured. Thus White's two main prospects are in the center and along the f-file. If he is successful in achieving both goals, his position will be much the better one.

Is there anything wrong with White's plans? Exactly the most obvious things: he is sacrificing a valuable pawn, and he is simultaneously weakening his King position.

2 ...	exf4!

In general, the best way to cope with a true gambit is to accept it. By "true gambit" I mean an offer of material that is not expected to be recaptured in the normal course of play. In such situations, the attacker is willing to accept some risks, and the defender should not flinch either. Here Black gains a pawn and weakens White's Kingside. Shouldn't Black be satisfied to achieve all this in only two moves?

For those who don't want to accept the risks associated with taking the pawn, Part Eight of this book discusses the other possibilities.

3 ♘f3

This is by far White's most usual method in the King's Gambit Accepted. The Knight is developed to its preferred central location and prevents a check by Black's Queen on h4.

Nevertheless, developing the King Bishop first with **3 ♗c4** (the Bishop's Gambit) is equally good. The Bishop is immediately mobilized on its most active diagonal, where it aims at f7 and makes Black's ... d7-d5 central counter more difficult to achieve. White doesn't have to worry about the immediate 3 ... ♕h4+ because the Queen will later be chased back with a gain of time for White. This was well demonstrated in the interesting game between Bobby Fischer and Larry Evans (U.S. Championship, 1963/64): 3 ... ♕h4+ 4 ♔f1 d6 5 ♘c3 ♗e6 6 ♕e2 c6 7 ♘f3 ♕e7 8 d4 ♗xc4 9 ♕xc4 g5 and now by undermining Black's Kingside with 10 h4! White can obtain the advantage; for instance, 10 ... g4 11 ♘e1 ♗h6 12 ♘d3.

Instead of wasting time with moves such as 3 ... ♕h4+, Black does best with the developing move **3 ... ♘f6!**, which attacks the e-pawn and prepares for the advance ... d7-d5 after the normal moves **4 ♘c3 c6.**

After 3 ♗c4 ♘f6 4 ♘c3 c6

This is the most important position in the Bishop's Gambit variation. No matter what White does, Black will be able to play ... d7-d5 with good prospects. Three possibilities:

1) **5 ♗b3** d5 6 exd5 cxd5 7 d4 ♗d6 8 ♘ge2 0-0 9 0-0 g5! 10 ♘xd5 ♘c6, and Black's Kingside pawn majority, due to its cramping effect, is equal in value to White's majority on the Queenside.

2) **5 d4** ♗b4 6 ♗d3 d5 7 e5 ♗g5 8 ♘f3 ♘e4 with equal chances.

3) **5 ♕f3?!** d5! 6 exd5 ♗d6! 7 d3 ♗g4 8 ♕f2 0-0 9 ♗xf4 ♖e8+ and Black will recover the pawn and still keep attacking chances; for instance, 10 ♔f1 b5 11 ♗b3 b4 12 ♘ce2 ♘xd5.

3 ... d5

At this moment Black has to make a fundamental decision. The basic choices are *(1)* to try to hold on to the extra pawn through thick and thin; *(2)* to complete Kingside development in a solid manner; *(3)* to develop the Kingside rapidly, giving priority to attaining counter-chances and not worrying that this might cost a pawn or two. The text move follows the latter approach, and we'll have more to say about it later on. First, we will discuss the other logical approaches.

1) **3 ... g5** immediately signifies that Black intends to hold on to his pawn. This approach is theoretically fine once White has played ♘f3, since Black has the possibility of playing ... g5-g4, hoping to gain time by forcing White's Knight to move. Often, however, White sacrifices his King Knight, when the game can become exceedingly complicated. The variations after 3 ... g5 are in fact the most complex ones in the King's Gambit Accepted, and despite the tremendous amount of analysis that already exists, much is still uncertain. Because this variation demands an inordinate amount of theoretical knowledge, especially on Black's part, it is rarely played in modern tournaments.

A logical development after 3 ... g5 is **4 ♗c4**, bringing out the Bishop to aim at Black's vulnerable f7, and Black's reply is **4 ... ♗g7**, developing his Bishop in a central direction. The immediate **4 ... g4!?** is extremely risky for both sides.

An enormous body of theory shows that White must sacrifice his Knight by playing **5 0-0!** (the Muzio Gambit), and after **5 ... gxf3 6 ♕xf3** White has good attacking chances—but Black has an extra piece. The chances are roughly equal, but in "real life" a draw is the least likely result.

After **4 ♗c4 ♗g7**, the normal course is **5 0-0**, bringing the King to relative safety and getting ready for action along the f-file.

Position after 3 ... g5
4 ♗c4 ♗g7 5 0-0

Now the usual continuation is **5 ... h6** (the g-pawn and the g5-square need solid protection) **6 d4** (developing while gaining central control) **6 ... ♘e7** (completing the development of the minor pieces on the Kingside and preparing to castle, given time) **7 g3!**, going immediately for action along the f-file. White's last move sets a trap: the obvious **7 ... fxg3?** is refuted by the sacrifice **8 ♘xg5! hxg5 9 ♗xf7+** with a killing attack after **9 ... ♔f8**; for instance,

10 e5, 10 ♗xg5, and 10 ♘h5 + ♔g8 11 ♕f3 are all good.

But Black avoids the trap with **7 ... d5!** (developing and counterattacking at the same time) **8 exd5 fxg3 9 ♘e5!** (White cannot tarry; after 9 hxg3 ♘f5! White has no compensation for his weakened Kingside) **9 ... gxh2 + 10 ♔h1!** (to utilize Black's h-pawn as a shield for the King; the materialistic 10 ♔xh2? is wrong, since White's King would be too exposed) **10 ... 0-0!**.

Black has withstood the first charge, he is two pawns ahead, and White's King position is hardly comfortable. Still, White can create further complications with 11 ♘xf7!?, leaving the ultimate result of the game very much in doubt.

2) **3 ... ♘f6** looks like a desirable way of developing the Knight. However, after **4 e5!** the Knight must move, and it has no fully satisfactory place to go. After 4 ... ♘e4 5 d3! ♘g5 6 ♗xf4 White has recovered the gambit pawn and has the superior central position. If **4 ... ♘h5**, then **5 ♗e2!** makes the Knight very uncomfortable on the edge of the board. For instance: 5 ... d6 6 0-0 dxe5 7 ♘xe5 ♕d4 + 8 ♔h1 ♘f6 (8 ... ♕xe5?! is worse—after 9 ♗xh5 Black's uncastled King is in big trouble, the immediate threat being 10 ♖e1, winning the Queen) 9 ♘d3 ♗d6 10 c3 ♕b6 11 ♘xf4 0-0 12 d4.

Position after 12 d4

White has recovered his pawn and he has the superior center and good attacking chances along the f-file—which is just about what White wants in the King's Gambit.

3) **3 ... ♗e7** is a more modest and successful way of developing the Kingside than 3 ... ♘f6. By threatening a Bishop check at h4—*at the appropriate moment*—Black is able to develop his King Knight without the disadvantages of the 3 ... ♘f6 variation.

The thematic next move for White is **4 ♗c4**, developing the Bishop to its most active square. After the unassuming 4 ♘c3, Black should eschew the tempting 4 ... ♗h4 + ?! since after 5 ♔e2! White's King will be safe enough and Black will have to lose more time to get his King Bishop to a useful location. Black's best plan after 4 ♘c3 is the developing 4 ... ♔f6!, which is similar to the line after 4 ♗c4.

The best moves after 4 ♗c4 are **4 ... ♘f6!** (it's questionable here too whether Black gains anything by 4 ... ♕h4+ 5 ♔f1!) **5 e5** (after 5 ♘c3, Black has the effective center-clearing 5 ... ♘xe4! with the idea of recovering the piece after 6 ♘xe4 d5) **5 ... ♘g4!**.

**Position after 3 ... ♗e7
4 ♗c4 ♘f6 5 e5 ♘g4**

Here, in contrast to the previous line, the Knight can go to an active square. The attempt to chase it away by 6 h3? fails to 6 ... ♗h4+, since after 7 ♔f1 ♘f2 8 ♕e1 ♘xh1 9 ♕xh4 ♘g3+ the Knight escapes with its bounty.

Best play in the diagram position is **6 0-0 ♘c6**, attacking the e-pawn and setting a trap. If White protects his pawn with the Rook, he gets a surprise: 7 ♖e1? ♗c5+! 8 d4 ♘xd4! 9 ♘xd4 ♕h4 and White is defenseless against the dual threats of 10 ... ♗xd4+ 11 ♕xd4 ♕xe1+ and 10 ... ♕xh2+.

After **7 d4 d5!** Black has at least

full equality whether White retreats the Bishop or plays 8 exd6 ♗xd6 9 ♖e1+ ♘e7.

4) 3 ... d6 is a flexible move first recommended by Bobby Fischer in the 1960's. Black establishes a measure of central influence and will try to hold on to the f-pawn with a subsequent ... g7-g5. Typical play is **4 ♗c4 h6** (guarding the g5-square and preparing ... g7-g5; Black doesn't have to worry about the preventive 5 h4?! by White since that would seriously weaken White's Kingside and Black could then effectively play the simple 5 ... ♘f6) **5 d4 g5 6 0-0 ♗g7**.

**After 3 ... d6 4 ♗c4 h6 5 d4 g5
6 0-0 ♗g7**

Another complicated, extremely unbalanced position. If White now plays the safe 7 c3, Black should develop the Queen Knight with 7 ... ♘c6. If White immediately tries to open lines with 7 g3!?, then Black should aim for counterplay in the center with 7 ... ♘c6 8 gxf4 g4!. In either case, an objective evaluation is tough to make. The King's Gambit Accepted is a fun opening for those with strong nerves and little concern for the opinions of opening theoreticians!

Now back to the 3 ... d5 of our main line.

After 1 e4 e5 2 f4 exf4 3 ♘f3 d5

The move 3 ... d5 opens the Queen Bishop's diagonal with a gain of time. Obviously, White can't ignore the attack on his e-pawn, and pushing by with 4 e5?! allows Black to establish strong central pressure at no cost: after 4 ... g5! 5 h3?! ♘h6! 6 d4 ♘f5 Black has a good extra pawn and the better chances (as has been known since the game Gunsberg-Pillsbury, Vienna 1903). Therefore, White's only sensible move is to capture.

4   exd5   ♘f6!

Remember that Black's primary objective in this variation is to achieve rapid and sound development of the Kingside, even if this might cost a little material. 4 ... ♕xd5? is completely contrary to this spirit, and, to prove it, White obtains the better development and the better chances as follows: 5 ♘c3 ♕e6+ 6 ♗e2 ♗d6 7 0-0 ♘e7 8 d4 0-0 9 ♘g5.

Apart from the text move, only 4 ... ♗d6 conforms to the spirit of the variation, and, in fact, after 5 ♗b5+ c6! it would most likely transpose into our main line.

5   ♗b5+

White's basic choice is between this check and protecting the newly gained d-pawn. There are three ways of accomplishing the latter and all of them deserve notice.

1) **5 c4** is by far the firmest way. Unless Black reacts very energetically, White's center will give him the advantage. Therefore the required move is **5 ... c6!** and after **6 dxc6?!** ♘xc6 7 d4 ♗g4 Black has a strong attacking position. To hold on to the d-pawn White will have to play 8 d5 ♗xf3 9 ♕xf3 ♘e5 10 ♕xf4, but after 10 ... ♗d6! followed by castling, Black will have excellent attacking prospects against White's uncastled King. Instead of 6 dxc6?!, the safer move is **6 d4,** but Black still has good chances for some advantage after the simple 6 ... cxd5 or 6 ... ♗b4+. Overall, it must be concluded that White hasn't time for the materialistic 5 c4?!.

2) **5 ♗c4** develops a piece while giving the d-pawn some protection, and it enables White to castle. Black has nothing better than to recover the d-pawn, and after 5 ... ♘xd5 6 0-0 ♗e6 7 ♗b3! the chances are about equal—if Black plays the sound developing move 7 ... ♗e7!. The overeager 7 ... ♗d6?! allows White to gain time with 8 c4! ♘e7 9 d4 ♘g6 10 c5!, and this gave White the advantage in the game Bronstein-I. Zaitsev, U.S.S.R. 1969. Black soon fell into a trap and lost quickly: 10 ... ♗e7 11 ♗xe6 fxe6 12 ♖e1 0-0 13 ♖xe6 ♗xc5? 14 ♕b3!! ♗xd4+ 15 ♘xd4 ♕xd4+ 16 ♗e3! and Black resigned. No matter what Black might have played, White's Rook would have discovered check on the next move to win Black's Queen.

Position after 16 ♗e3!

3) **5 ♘c3** starts developing the Queenside while giving modest protection to the d-pawn. If Black now cavalierly passes up winning the pawn back and plays 5 ... ♗d6?!, White keeps the pawn easily with 6 ♗c4 0-0 7 0-0 ♘bd7 8 d4!. With his King safe and a superiority in the center, White would have a nice advantage. Therefore Black should play the simple **5 ... ♘xd5** 6 ♘xd5 ♕xd5 7 d4 ♗e7!. Then 8 ♗xf4?? loses the Bishop after 8 ... ♕e4+. And after 8 c4 ♕e4+ 9 ♗e2 ♘c6 10 0-0 ♗f5 11 ♖e1 0-0-0! Black has sufficient counterchances along the d-file.

If White is satisfied with a sound, equal position, then 5 ♗c4 and 5 ♘c3 are the best choices. Of course, when White plays the King's Gambit he often wants a lot more. In the spirit of such adventurousness is the text move, 5 ♗b5+.

After 1 e4 e5 2 f4 exf4 3 ♘f3 d5 4 exd5 ♘f6 5 ♗b5+

White completes the development of his Kingside with gain of time— that's why he gives this check. If

Black is too slow, White will get what he wants. For example, 5 ... ♘bd7?! 6 c4! a6 7 ♗xd7+ ♗xd7 8 0-0! and White has gained domination of the center at no cost. Or 5 ... ♗d7?! 6 ♗c4! and now, since Black's Bishop is shielding the White d-pawn, if Black wants to win back the pawn he must misplace the Queen with 6 ... ♕e7+. White then has an excellent chance of exploiting this with 7 ♗e2! ♘xd5 8 0-0! followed by 9 c4! and 10 d4.

5 ...   c6!

Avoiding any loss of time and assuring smooth, rapid development. Obviously, White's next move is forced.

6   dxc6   ♘xc6!

Capturing this way is not that obvious, yet it becomes clearly the best when we keep in mind the overall objective of Black's opening strategy in this variation: *smooth, rapid development.* Therefore, less effective is **6 ... bxc6?! 7 ♗c4** because after **7 ... ♗d6** and the annoying reply **8 ♕e2+!**, Black has only the unattractive choices **8 ... ♗e7** (losing time), **8 ... ♕e7** (leading to an undesirable exchange of Queens), and **8 ... ♔f8** (losing the castling privilege). Centralizing the King Knight with **7 ... ♘d5** is somewhat better, so that after White's d2-d4, Black's Knight has access to e3. However, straight-

forward and effective development by **8 ♘c3!** (preventing 8 ... ♗d6) **8 ... ♗e7 9 0-0 0-0 10 d4** leaves White with the advantage since **10 ... ♘e3?! 11 ♗xe3 fxe3 12 ♕d3** signs the death warrant for Black's brand-new e-pawn.

7   d4

Taking control of the center and threatening 8 ♗xf4. Again Black must be most consistent in his play.

7   ...   ♗d6!

Only so. The f-pawn must be protected and the King must castle. 7 ... ♕a5+? 8 ♘c3 ♗b4 is an unaffordable loss of time since after 9 0-0! ♗xc3 10 ♕e2+ White will have a strong center and marvelous attacking prospects without cost.

8   ♕e2+

An attempt to make it more difficult for Black to complete his Kingside development. Quieter play results from **8 0-0 0-0 9 ♘bd2 ♗g4**

10 ♘c4 ♗c7. White can then solidify his center with 11 c3 or further damage Black's pawn formation with 11 ♗xc6. After 11 c3 Black should respond 11 ... ♘e7!, threatening 12 ... a6 13 ♗a4 b5, and after 11 ♗xc6 bxc6 12 ♕d3 the logical move for Black is the centralizing 12 ... ♕d5. In either case, material is even and the position essentially balanced, and thus the chances are equal.

8 ... ♗e6!

Only so! The last thing that Black can afford is to move anything backward! Since he has the inferior pawn formation, his compensation must be found in rapid development and the resulting attacking chances.

Black has no need to worry about 9 c4? 0-0! 10 d5 because of 10 ... ♗g4!, threatening to win the Queen with 11 ... ♖e8. Therefore, White would not have time to capture the Knight, and his 9th and 10th moves would turn out to have been a loss of development time that has seriously

compromised his position.

Since White wants to exploit his superior pawn formation in due course, it makes sense for him to try to limit Black's attacking chances. In this connection, **9 ♗c4!** appears to be quite logical. White would welcome the opportunity to exchange his do-nothing Bishop for Black's potentially very strong one. Although this move is apparently not considered by books on opening theory, it leads to a sound position for White and chances for exploiting Black's pawn weaknesses in the middlegame. From an objective standpoint, the position after 9 ♗c4! must be rated as approximately equal.

Instructive Game No. 1

White: W. Hartston
Black: B. Spassky

Hastings 1965/66

1	e4	e5
2	f4	exf4
3	♘f3	d5
4	exd5	♘f6
5	♗b5 +	c6
6	dxc6	♘xc6
7	d4	♗d6
8	♕e2 +	♗e6
9	♘e5?!	

This certainly looks logical, since it carries the dual threats 10 ♘xc6 bxc6 11 ♗xc6 + and 10 ♗xf4. The fundamental drawback of the move, however, is that it neither advances

White's development nor impedes Black's. Since White is already behind in development in an open position, 9 ♘e5 cannot be the best he has.

9 ... 0-0!

Speed of development is far more important here than to worry about a pawn.

10 ♗xc6

White may as well execute his plan; otherwise he'll have no compensation for his backward development. Clearly worse is 10 ♘xc6? bxc6 11 ♗xc6, for after 11 ... ♖c8! Black's attacking chances would be even stronger than they are in the game.

10	...	bxc6
11	♗xf4	♘d5!
12	♗g3	

The greedy 12 ♘xc6? gets punished by 12 ... ♕h4+ 13 g3

♘xf4! 14 gxh4 ♘xe2 15 ♔xe2 ♗d5 and White, deservedly, loses his Knight.

12 ... f6!

Time is of the essence! If now 13 ♘xc6 ♗xg3+ 14 hxg3 ♕d6 and Black threatens both the Knight and 15 ... ♕xg3+. Therefore, the brave Knight must beat an abject retreat.

13	♘f3	♗xg3+
14	hxg3	♖e8!

Black has more than full compensation for the pawn and threatens a decisive attack by moving his Bishop. Even from a strictly materialistic standpoint White is not really ahead a *full* pawn, since the isolated and doubled g-pawns seriously devalue White's pawn count.

15 ♔f2

Castling may look more logical but then White would have more trouble protecting the g3-pawn. Consider this variation: 15 0-0 ♗f5 16 ♕f2 ♘e3 17 ♖c1 ♕d6! threatening 18 ... ♘g4 followed by 19 ... ♕xg3.

15	...	♗f5
16	♕c4	♔h8
17	♘c3	♘e3
18	♕c5	♘g4+!
19	♔g1	♕d7

Keeping White in a complete bind and preparing to double Rooks on the e-file.

20 ♖f1?

Much too defeatist an attitude. The required move is 20 ♖c1!. Then White would at least have a pawn for his trouble. After the text move he has nothing and can expect nothing—except more trouble.

20	...	♗xc2
21	♖h4	♘e3
22	♖c1	g5

Black can easily afford this

weakening of his Kingside since White is in no position to take advantage of it.

23	♖h6	♗g6
24	♘a4	♘g4
25	♖h3	♕e6!
26	♕c3	

He must prevent 26 ... ♕e3+, but 26 ♖e1? allows 26 ... ♕xe1+ 27 ♘xe1 ♖xe1 mate.

26	...	♕xa2
27	♘c5	♖e3
28	♕d2	♖ae8!
	White resigns	

Already a pawn down and having to face the coming 29 ... ♖e2, White sees no reason to prolong his agony.

Instructive Game No. 2

White: Gross
Black: J. Plachetka

Czechoslovakia 1972

1	e4	e5
2	f4	exf4
3	♘f3	d5
4	exd5	♘f6
5	♗b5+	c6
6	dxc6	♘xc6
7	d4	♗d6
8	♕e2+	♗e6
9	♘g5?!	

With the logical plan of exchanging Black's Bishop, perhaps also gaining a pawn in the process.

However, the absence of the Knight considerably weakens his Kingside. Therefore the suggested 9 ♗c4! is better.

9	...	0-0!
10	♘xe6	fxe6
11	♗xc6	bxc6
12	0-0	

White's strategy seems to have triumphed. Since he is threatening both 13 ♕xe6+ and 13 ♗xf4, he is sure to win a pawn.

12	...	♕c7!

"Be my guest!" says Black. The f-pawn is the most troublesome one to White and the one that hinders the effective development of his Bishop, and it is therefore the one that Black must hold.

13	♘d2?!

White has been "psyched." Although after 13 ♕xe6+ ♔h8 14 ♕h3 (the threat was 14 ... f3! 15 g3?! ♗xg3!) 14 ... ♖ae8 Black has full compensation for the pawn, White would still have good defensive resources after 15 ♘d2.

13	...	e5!

Now Black has a strong initiative on the Kingside and in the center, and it cost him nothing. However, White defends well and manages to keep his disadvantage to a minimum.

14	dxe5	♗xe5
15	♘f3!	♗d6
16	♗d2!	♖ae8
17	♕c4+	♔h8
18	♖ae1!	♕b6+
19	♔h1	♕b5

Surprisingly, Black wants to switch to an endgame in which, with his Queenside pawns straightened out, he will have a slight advantage due to his more active position. The complicated middlegame would be maintained with 19 ... ♘d5!?.

20	♕xb5	cxb5

21 ♘g5

White threatens 22 ♖xe8 ♖xe8 23 ♘f7+, or if 21 ... ♔g8?! 22 ♘e6 is annoying. With the following Rook exchange Black prevents all of White's plans.

21	...	♖xe1!
22	♖xe1	h5

22 ... h6! is sounder, but the text move tempts White to win a pawn.

23 ♘e6?!

Either 23 ♗c3 or 23 h3 would give White approximate equality.

23	...	♖e8
24	♖e2	♔g8
25	♘xf4	

The better capture is 25 ♗xf4!

♖xe6 26 ♖xe6 ♗xf4 27 ♖a6 and the active position of the Rook should allow White to draw without much difficulty.

25	...	♘e4!
26	♔g1	♗c5+

A tricky moment. Any King move loses: 27 ♔f1? ♘xd2+ 28 ♖xd2 ♖f8 pinning and winning the Knight, and for 27 ♔h1? see the game. White must play 27 ♗e3 and be satisfied with the inferior endgame after 27 ... ♘c3! 28 bxc3 ♖xe3! 29 ♔f1 ♖xc3.

27	♔h1?	♘f2+
28	♔g1?!	♖xe2!
29	♘xe2	♘e4+
30	♔f1	♘xd2+
31	♔e1	♘c4
	White resigns.	

Part Eight
King's Gambit Declined

Edmar Mednis

White	Black
1 e4	e5
2 f4	

As discussed in Part Seven, there are sound *chess* reasons why the King's Gambit should be accepted. However, other factors may come into play. Some players like rather clear strategic positions; for them the King's Gambit Accepted may seem too obscure and complicated. Then there are players who don't like being pressed and in fact savor positions which offer immediate chances to counterattack. Both these types of players may do better in a practical game—for psychological reasons—by *not* accepting the gambit.

There are two basic approaches in declining the gambit. One way is simply to do your own thing in developing your pieces and watching the center. The following three lines are playable:

1) **2 ... d6** protects the e-pawn and ensures some central presence. If now 3 ♘f3, Black can play 3 ... exf4 and transpose into the 2 ... exf4 3 ♘f3 d6 variation of the King's Gambit Accepted. Stronger,

therefore, is **3 ♘c3!** and after **3 ... ♘f6**, only then **4 ♘f3**. To protect the e-pawn Black plays **4 ... ♘c6 5 ♗b5 ♗d7**; however, after **6 d3!** White threatens the simple capture 7 ♗xc6 followed by 8 fxe5. Therefore, Black has nothing better than 6 ... exf4, and after the logical moves **7 ♗xf4 ♗e7 8 0-0 0-0 9 d4** White has achieved the indicated goals of the King's Gambit: central control and play along the f-file. Overall, White has a nice advantage.

2) **2 ... ♗c5** followed by ... d7-d6 is a more promising plan because the Bishop is more active on c5 than on e7. Consistent play for both sides is now **3 ♘f3** (3 fxe5?? ♕h4+) **3 ... d6 4 ♘c3**. An alternate plan is to try to get in d2-d4 by playing 4 c3 or first 4 fxe5 dxe5 and then 5 c3. (Of course, 5 ♘xe5?? is a blunder which gives Black's Queen access to h4 for a most unpleasant check: 5 ... ♕h4+ 6 g3 ♕xe4+ 7 ♕e2 ♕xh1, and, although White wins the Black Rook on h8 with 8 ♘g6+ ♘e7 9 ♘xh8, his chances of extricating the Knight after, say, 9 ... ♗h3, are remote.) After either 4 c3 or 4 fxe5 dxe5 5 c3, Black should play the developing ... ♘f6; in either case White is only slightly better. With 4 ♘c3 White wants to complete his development first.

After 2 ... ♗c5 3 ♘f3 d6 4 ♘c3

Play normally continues **4 ... ♘f6 5 ♗c4 ♘c6 6 d3**. The two King Bishops are of equivalent value, but White's pressure on the center and his chances along the f-file give him a slight edge. One possibility: 6 ... ♗g4 7 ♘a4 ♘d4 8 ♘xc5 dxc5 9 c3 ♘xf3+ 10 gxf3 ♗h5 11 ♕e2 and White has retained his central superiority and a slight advantage.

3) **2 ... ♘f6** is an attempt to counterattack while developing. However, with **3 fxe5 ♘xe4 4 ♘f3 d5** (the somewhat inferior endgame Black gets after 4 ... ♘g5!? 5 d4 ♘xf3+ 6 ♕xf3 ♕h4+ 7 ♕f2 is the best he has, although it is not an attractive prospect) **5 d3! ♘c5 6 d4 ♘e4 7 ♗d3** White

has a clear central superiority, harmonious development, and excellent attacking chances—and thus the considerably better prospects.

The second approach in declining the King's Gambit is to launch a counteroffensive.

2 ...   d5!?

This is known as the Falkbeer Countergambit. Its rationale is as follows: since 2 f4 has not contributed to White's development and has weakened his King position, Black is justified in making an audacious advance in the center. In general, Black will be aiming for very fast piece development, and he is prepared to pay the price of a pawn or two. According to the latest theoretical evaluations, and applying the strictest standards, the Falkbeer is not a *completely* sound gambit. However, in order to demonstrate this, White must navigate successfully through some exceedingly complex variations. One misstep and Black is on top. In this opening missteps are very easy to make, and that's what Black is counting on. In actual practice, Black's results are much better than the theoretical predictions!

3 exd5!

The only way to try to punish Black. If White wants to avoid complications and is satisfied with equality, he can start developing with 3 ♘f3 dxe4 4 ♘xe5.

3 ... e4!?

The only consistent followup: Black tries to hinder White's development and wants to show that 2 f4 was a Kingside weakening and a loss of time. Of course, 3 ... exf4 is quite playable, but it has no independent value since the most likely continuation, 4 ♘f3 ♘f6, transposes into the main line of the King's Gambit Accepted.

On the other hand, 3 ... c6?! is too slow. True, Black gets a tremendous lead in development if White is greedy: 4 dxc6? ♘xc6 5 d3 ♗c5 6 ♘c3 ♘f6 7 ♘f3 0-0. However, after the developing move **4 ♘c3!** White has a safe advantage, since 4 ... cxd5 5 fxe5 d4 6 ♘e4 ♕d5 7 ♗d3! gives him a very strong attack if Black takes the e-pawn.

4 d3!

Black's annoying outpost must be challenged and eliminated. Everything else is inferior:

1) 4 c4?! c6! 5 ♘c3 ♘f6 leaves open the question of how White is going to develop his Kingside. The foolhardy pawn grab 6 dxc6? ♘xc6 gives Black a big lead in development.

2) 4 ♗b5 + ?! c6! 5 dxc6 bxc6! 6 ♗c4 ♗c5 7 ♘e2 ♘f6 again gives Black excellent compensation for the pawn, since White's King will be very uncomfortable in the middle of the board.

3) 4 ♘c3 ♘f6 5 ♕e2 ♗f5 also leaves White in a quandary as to how to proceed.

4 ... ♘f6

Development! 4 ... exd3?! just furthers *White's* development while leaving Black a pawn down: after 5 ♕xd3 ♘f6 6 ♘c3 ♗c5 7 ♗d2 0-0 8 0-0-0 ♘bd7 9 g3! ♘b6 10 ♗g2, and White is better both positionally and materially. Also questionable is 4 ... ♕xd5, since 5

♘d2!? exd3 6 ♗xd3! eliminates Black's center and sets the trap 6 ... ♕xg2?? 7 ♗e4 ♕g4 (forced) 8 ♕xg4 ♗xg4 9 ♗xb7, and Black's Queen Rook disappears.

5 dxe4!

The simplest move and the strongest one. Black's center disappears, and White's pin on the e-file will be difficult for Black to handle. The other possibilities are:

1) **5 ♘c3?!** needlessly allows the pin 5 ... ♗b4. White should now risk the complicated line 6 dxe4 ♘xe4 7 ♕d4 ♕e7 8 ♗e2, in which his chances for equality are good. But the seemingly safe 6 ♗d2?! is dangerous, because of 6 ... e3!! 7 ♗xe3 0-0!. How quickly White can go under is shown by the game Rohde-Brasket, New York 1977: 8 ♕f3?! (8 ♗d2! is better) 8 ... ♖e8 9 ♗e2 ♗g4 10 ♕g3 ♗xe2 11 ♘gxe2 ♕e7! 12 ♔f2 ♕xe3+! 13 ♕xe3 ♘g4+ and Black wins a piece and the game.

2) **5 ♕e2** sets up the pin immediately, but the Queen is awkwardly placed here and Black can either play the simple 5 ... ♕xd5 or 5 ... ♗f5, or he can offer a promising pawn sacrifice with 5 ... ♗g4 6 ♕e3 ♘xd5!? 7 ♕xe4+ ♗e7 8 f5 ♘f6 9 ♕xb7 ♘bd7. After Black's imminent recovery of the f-pawn he will be only one pawn behind and as compensation will have a substantial lead in development.

3) **5 ♘d2** does achieve the liquidation of Black's e-pawn after 5 ... exd3 6 ♗d3, yet the Knight's clumsy location shows up after 6 ... ♘xd5!. If now 7 ♕e2+ Black has the luxury of playing either 7 ... ♗e7 or 7 ... ♕e7, in either case with very comfortable equality.

5 ...   ♘xe4
6 ♘f3!

This normal developing move is by far White's strongest continuation; it prevents a potential ... ♕h4+ by Black and keeps open the possibility of setting up a pin on the e-file with ♕e2. It is not the most obvious move, however, for now Black's possible reply 6 ... ♝c5 looks very strong. But we will see that White need not fear that move.

Everything else is worse:

1) The immediate **6 ♕e2?!** fails after the simple 6 ... ♕xd5 7 ♘d2 f5 and White will be lucky to equalize.

2) **6 ♝e3** gives Black a choice: he can play for a promising attack with 6 ... ♝d6!? 7 ♘f3 0-0 or he can recover the pawn with the complicated-looking 6 ... ♕h4+ 7 g3 ♘xg3 8 ♘f3 ♕e7! and wind up in an even endgame after 9 hxg3 ♕xe3+ 10 ♕e2 ♕xe2+ 11 ♝xe2 ♝g4.

6 ...   ♝c5

The only move that makes sense, for otherwise Black remains a pawn behind and with nothing to show for it.

7 ♕e2

The critical position: it requires very careful analysis to be sure of who is actually better. White's King seems threatened by Black's minor pieces, but it turns out that the pin along the e-file is the most important element in the position. Black now has five moves that look reasonable, but four of them are unsatisfactory:

1) **7 ... ♝f2+?** looks great, but it's refuted like this: 8 ♔d1 ♕xd5+ 9 ♘fd2! f5 10 ♘c3 ♕d4 11 ♘xe4 fxe4 12 c3 ♕e3 13 ♕h5+! (now it is White's turn to attack; of course 13 ♘xe4 is not bad, leading to a pawn-up endgame) 13 ... ♔f8 14 ♝c4 ♕xf4 15 ♕d5! and White's attack wins, since he is threatening both 16 ♕d8 mate and 16 ♘xe4 followed by 17 ♖f1.

2) **7 ... 0-0?** doesn't lead to an attack for Black after 8 ♕xe4 ♖e8 9 ♘e5 f6—it leads to an attack for *White* after 10 ♘c3! fxe5 11 fxe5.

3) **7 ... ♕xd5?** also entangles Black in problems on the e-file: 8 ♘fd2! f5 9 ♘c3 ♕d4 10 ♘cxe4 fxe4 11 ♘b3! and the best move Black has, 11 ... ♕d5, leads to a horrible position a pawn down after 12 ♘xc5 ♕xc5 13 ♕xe4+.

4) **7 ... f5?!** is also insufficient, since by means of 8 ♝e3! ♕xd5 9 ♝xc5 ♕xc5 10 ♘c3 White again exploits the pin with no risk to himself, and obtains the advantage.

Therefore, the only way for Black to stay in the game is the fifth possibility:

7... ♗f5

This not only protects the Knight but also sets a sophisticated trap. If White gets greedy with 8 ̄g4? he succeeds in winning the piece but loses the game: 8 ... 0-0! 9 gxf5 ♖e8! and Black has a devastating attack against White's uncastled King. One example: 10 ♗g2 ♘f2 11 ♘e5 ♘xh1 12 ♗xh1 ♘d7 13 ♘c3 f6 and Black will have a material advantage to go with his positional one.

8 ♘c3!

Developing while attacking is the correct approach. Black must defend the attacked Knight. The counterpin 8 ... ♗b4? loses the Bishop after 9 ♕b5 + , and the sacrifice 8 ... 0-0? is inadequate after 9 ♘xe4 ♖e8 10 ♘e5.

8 ... ♕e7
9 ♗e3!

This move, though inherently logical, is still far from obvious. White wants to develop his pieces,

and he wants to neutralize the diagonal of Black's dark-square Bishop; however, the move leads to a materially equal endgame of which the correct evaluation is at first glance uncertain. In fact, as considerable practical experience and theoretical analyses have shown, the endgame is clearly superior for White. Whereas the first person to play 9 ♗e3! must have done so with some trepidation, we can play it with full confidence!

Again, because of the open nature of the position, there is no time for petty greed with 9 ♘xe4?! ♗xe4 10 c4; Black opens the position even more with 10 ... c6! and has plenty of compensation for the pawn.

9 ... ♗xe3

Another interesting move, which in the end is equivalent to the text, is 9 ... ♘xc3 10 ♗xc5 ♘xe2 11 ♗xe7 ♘xf4, and now White's strongest line is to keep Black's King from castling with 12 ♗a3!. White obtains very strong pressure against Black's position no matter what Black plays: 12 ... ♘d7 13 0-0-0 ♗e4 (13 ... 0-0-0? loses to 14 ♖d4! ♘g6 15 g4!) 14 ♘g5! ♗xd5 gives White the pleasant choice between 15 ♖e1 + , 15 ♗b5, 15 ♖d4, or even the audacious 15 g3!? that Bronstein played against Tal in Riga 1968. Grabbing the d-pawn immediately with 12 ... ♘xd5 also leads to a terrific attack for White: 13 0-0-0 c6 14 ♘g5! ♘d7 15 ♗c4! ♗e6 16 ♖he1.

10 ♕xe3

White now threatens simply to castle on the Queenside, after which he will have a great position to go with his extra pawn on d5. Therefore, Black has nothing better than to enter the endgame with 10 ... ♘xc3 11 ♕xe7+ ♔xe7 12 bxc3. I'll have more to say about this endgame in the notes to the instructive game which follows.

The overall conclusion—and there is no "poetic" justice in it at all—is that, theoretically, the very interesting, creative, and daring Falkbeer Countergambit is not fully satisfactory because, with *perfect* play, White can obtain the better *endgame*.

Instructive Game

White: D. Bronstein
Black: Vaisman

Sandomierz 1976

1	e4	e5
2	f4	d5
3	exd5	e4

4	d3	♘f6
5	dxe4!	♘xe4
6	♘f3	♗c5

There are no prospects in 6 ... ♗f5?! since White plays 7 ♗e3!, preventing Black's Bishop from stationing itself on c5. Black then has no compensation for the missing pawn, and, in the game Alekhine-Tarrasch, St. Petersburg 1914, an attempt to force matters with 7 ... c6 8 ♗c4! b5?! 9 ♗b3 c5 led to an immediate catastrophe for Black after 10 d6! c4 11 ♕d5!.

7	♕e2	♗f5
8	♘c3	♕e7
9	♗e3!	♗xe3
10	♕xe3	♘xc3
11	♕xe7+	♔xe7
12	bxc3	

This is the endgame I referred to earlier. At the moment White is a pawn up, and if Black does "nothing"—e.g., 12 ... ♘d7—White simply castles (13 0-0-0) and has a nice pawn in a nice position.

Therefore, Black must recover the pawn immediately. He has two ways of doing this, but each allows White to obtain a significant advantage in development. The simpler 12 ... ♗xc2 occurs in the game. The trickier alternative is 12 ... ♗e4. Then 13 c4?! ♗xf3 14 gxf3 ♘d7 leads to equal chances since Black's good Knight and much better pawn formation compensate him for the missing pawn. However, White obtains a very strong initiative with 13 ♘g5! ♗xd5 14 0-0-0. What is Black to do now? 14 ... ♗xa2? 15 c4 threatens to win the Bishop, so Black must immediately liberate it with 15 ... b5. Or if 14 ... ♖d8, then either 15 ♖e1+ or 15 c4 ♗e6 16 ♖xd8 is good for White. Or if 14 ... c6, then 15 ♗d3 carries the very unpleasant threat 16 ♖he1+. Finally, 14 ... ♗e6 15 ♘xe6 fxe6 16 ♗c4 followed by 17 ♖he1 will mean the loss of the e-pawn.

12	...	♗xc2
13	♔d2!	♗a4

Where should he put the Bishop? After 13 ... ♗g6 14 ♖e1+ ♔d8 15 ♘d4 White also has a very strong bind and Black has to watch out that his Bishop doesn't get trapped.

14 ♖e1+

Black now has no fully satisfactory location for his King. The lesser evil is 14 ... ♔d8 15 ♖e4 ♗e8, although after 16 ♗c4 b5 17 ♗b3

♘a6 18 ♖he1 White's pressure is very unpleasant.

14	...	♔d6?!

The King is very unsafe here.

15	♘g5!	♔xd5?!

Black is at least consistent. Although this leads to a forced loss, it gives Black the practical hope of coming out all right if White misplays the attack. Something like 15 ... ♗e8 would delay the end, but it would give Black little practical hope of anything.

16	♖e4!	♗e8

White is weaving a mating net that leads to decisive material gain. Black has little choice; for instance, 16 ... b5 merely encourages 17 c4+; 16 ... ♗c6 17 ♖e5+ ♔d6 18 ♘xf7+ costs a Rook; 16 ... ♗d7 17 ♗c4+ allows the attack to roll on.

17	♖d4+	♔c6

18 ♗e2!

With the Bishop and King Rook joining the attack, White will have four pieces hunting Black's solitary King. The end is near.

18	...	♘d7
19	♗f3+	♔b6
20	♖b1+	♔a5
21	♖xb7	h6
22	♖xc7	

Uncovering an attack on Black's Queen Rook.

22	...	♖b8
23	♘xf7	♗xf7
24	♖cxd7	**Black resigns**

The end is here. More than hopeless is 24 ... ♗e6 25 ♖xa7+ ♔b6 26 ♖xg7.

Part Nine
Vienna Game

Jack Peters

White	Black
1 e4	e5
2 ♘c3	

The Vienna Game has been undeservedly neglected by most grandmasters. The theoreticians have paid most attention to the exciting variations of the King's Gambit, the Giuoco Piano, and the Two Knights Defense, while the practical players have habitually relied on the Ruy Lopez. This gives the Vienna a unique standing: an ancient but unexplored opening!

The late American master Weaver Adams was one of the few champions of the Vienna Game. He used it as the basis for his "White to play and win" theory, but he was eventually frustrated by Black's sacrifice in the variation 1 e4 e5 2 ♘c3 ♘f6 3 ♗c4 ♘xe4!?. After his death, his disciples rehabilitated White's defense (!) in that critical variation, but the Vienna still did not catch on. Bent Larsen, who loves to experiment with unpopular openings, is the leading grandmaster who occasionally gives the Vienna a whirl (but he usually enters it by transposition from the Bishop's Opening). Spassky beat Korchnoi with the Vienna in a game of their 1977 match for the right to challenge Karpov for the World Championship.

White accomplishes several things with 2 ♘c3. He defends his e-pawn, seizes control of the central square d5, develops a Knight to a fine post, and keeps the option of playing either d2-d4 or f2-f4.

But 2 ♘c3, unlike 2 ♘f3, doesn't threaten anything. Therefore, Black is not forced to make a defensive move but can play either 2 ... ♘f6 or 2 ... ♘c6.

2 ...	♘f6

Often 2 ... ♘c6 leads to the same positions. If White selects 3 g3 or 3 ♗c4 there's little difference between 2 ... ♘c6 and 2 ... ♘f6. But if White tries **3 f4!?**, the differences are significant. Obviously, after 2 ... ♘c6 3 f4 Black can't reply 3 ... d5, as he can after 2 ... ♘f6 3 f4 (discussed later).

Position after 2 ... ♘c6 3 f4

If Black takes the pawn with 3 ... **exf4,** the game resembles the King's Gambit Accepted (Part 7). A popular continuation is **4 ♘f3 g5** (4 ... ♘f6 5 ♗c4 and later d2-d4 gives White a dominating center) **5 h4!?** g4 6 ♘g5 h6 7 ♘xf7 ♕xf7 8 d4. In this variation, known as the Hamppe-Allgaier Gambit, White will try a direct attack against Black's King. Avenues to the King are the f-file (after White captures the pawn on f4 and puts a Rook on f1) and the diagonal a2-g8. Logically, two of the best defensive plans are to plug the f-file, even temporarily (8 ... f3! 9 gxf3 ♗e7, threatening ... ♗xh4+), and to block the a2-g8 diagonal (8 ... d5! 9

♗xf4 ♗b4). Black's defense is difficult, but if he survives the onslaught he will surely win the game with his extra piece.

A different sacrifice can also give Black serious problems. After 4 ♘f3 g5 White can attack with **5 d4** (instead of 5 h4!?) **5 ... g4** (else 6 d5 gains time and space) **6 ♗c4!? gxf3 7 ♕xf3**. Indicative of White's chances is 7 ... ♗h6?! 8 0-0 ♘xd4 9 ♗xf7+ ♔xf7 10 ♕h5+ ♔g7 11 ♗xf4 ♗xf4 12 ♖xf4 ♘f6 13 ♕g5+ ♔f7 14 ♖af1, winning back one piece and retaining a tremendous attack. This variation was played in the famous match between MacDonnell (White) and Labourdonnais in 1835! The correct defense, however, is **7 ... d5!** 8 ♗xd5 ♕h4+ 9 g3 ♕g4. Notice how Black returns part of his material surplus to catch up in development and reduce White's threats.

Such all-out sacrificial attacks are not trusted by most of today's best players, but among amateurs they still claim victim after victim because one slip by Black is fatal. If you are worried about your ability to turn back an attack like this, you may prefer to answer 3 f4!? with **3 ... ♗c5.** White's natural reply 4 ♘f3 leads to the King's Gambit Declined (Part 8) after 4 ... d6. (The position usually arises from 1 e4 e5 2 f4 ♗c5 3 ♘f3 d6 4 ♘c3 ♘c6.) The alternative 4 fxe5 leaves Black with the attack after 4 ... d6! 5 exd6 ♕xd6 6 ♘f3

♗g4, since Black's lead in development seems more important than White's extra pawn. If White was planning to attack, he may not be able to make a satisfactory adjustment to having to defend instead!

After 2 ... ♘f6, White has several important choices.

Position after 2 ... ♘f6

3 ♗c4

We will consider 3 ♗c4 the main line. The other moves are 3 f4, 3 g3, and 3 ♘f3 ♘c6 (Four Knights Game, see Part 4).

The most aggressive choice is 3 ♗c4, placing the Bishop on the open a2-g8 diagonal, intensifying White's pressure on d5, and retaining options of f2-f4 or d2-d4.

With **3 f4** White challenges Black's center and hopes to open the f-file for his Rook. Black doesn't want to play 3 ... exf4? because of 4 e5, chasing the Knight back to g8, and 3 ... d6?! 4 ♘f3

followed by d2-d4 gives White the upper hand in the center and also confines Black's Bishop on f8.

The only strong reply to 3 f4 is **3 ... d5!**. If 4 exd5, Black can transpose to the King's Gambit Accepted with 4 ... exf4 (see Part 7) or the King's Gambit Declined with 4 ... e4 (see Part 8, under the move order 1 e4 e5 2 f4 d5 3 exd5 e4 4 ♘c3). The usual Vienna approach is **4 fxe5 ♘x4**.

After 3 f4 d5 4 fxe5 ♘xe4

Black's well-placed Knight at e4 makes up for White's strong pawn at e5. A very complicated line is **5 d3!?** ♕h4+ 6 g3 ♘xg3 7 ♘f3! ♕h5 8 ♘xd5!, when White probably has the better chances. But Black can safely avoid this wild variation with 5 ... ♘xc3 6 bxc3 ♗e7 7 ♘f3 0-0 8 d4 f6!. Exchanging the e-pawn should equalize. The pawn structure is almost symmetrical after 9 exf6 ♗xf6, and Black's pieces occupy good positions.

If **5 ♘f3**, Black again does best with straightforward development: 5 ... ♗e7 6 d4 0-0 7 ♗d3 f5!. If White doesn't capture the f-pawn en passant with 8 exf6, then Black's Knight on e4 will be unassailable. And 8 exf6 ♗xf6! solves all Black's problems. Black will gain time by ... ♘c6, attacking the pawn at d4. White can't win a pawn by 9 ♘xe4? dxe4 10 ♗xe4? because of 10 ... ♖e8, pinning the Bishop. After 8 exf6 ♗xf6, the open e- and f-files make Rook exchanges likely, and this increases the tendency of the game to end in a draw.

Completely different is **3 g3**.

Position after 3 g3

White does not plan to attack Black right away. In this variation, he's more concerned with setting up a solid position and postpones the struggle until the middlegame. Although this appears to be the feeblest of White's possibilities on the third move, it is the most popular among masters. Part of the reason is

that a master expects his opponent to know the correct replies to 3 ♗c4 and 3 f4, and they generally give Black equal chances. But 3 g3 has not yet been exhaustively analyzed, and thus Black is on his own at an earlier stage than in the other lines.

Black has a wide range of answers to 3 g3 because of the lack of a threat. As always, the pawn configuration in the center determines the further course of the game. Black has two overall strategies: to open the center with ... d7-d5 or to keep the center closed.

The idea behind **3 ... d5** is to exploit the lack of threat in White's second and third moves by gaining an advantage in the center. But after 4 exd5 ♘xd5 5 ♗g2 ♘xc3 6 bxc3, White's King Bishop has a fine diagonal, and the doubled pawns will prove helpful in supporting d2-d4. White also has a half-open b-file for his Rook, which will cooperate with his King Bishop to attack b7.

Nevertheless, Black's game is nearly equal. This was Korchnoi's choice as Black against Spassky in their 1977 match. Their game continued 6 ... ♗d6 7 ♘f3 0-0 8 0-0 c5?! (overly concerned about White's d2-d4) 9 d3 ♘c6 10 ♘d2!, reopening the diagonal. Spassky's Knight threatens to settle on e4 or c4. White has a slight edge here, and he later won the game. But 8 ... ♘c6! offers more resistance.

Black may reason that ... d7-d5 helps White by opening the diagonal for his King Bishop. If White's pawn remains at e4, his Bishop will be blocked and will be far less effective. I agree with this line of thinking and prefer **3 ... &c5** to 3 ... d5. Black will still find active posts for his pieces, and, by controlling d4 and preventing d2-d4, will have as much influence in the center as White does.

Position after 3 g3 &c5

After **4 &g2 &c6 5 &ge2 d6**, Black's options are still open. If White plays 6 0-0?!, Black can launch a promising attack with 6 ... h5!, utilizing his King Rook on its original square (and castling on the Queenside). If White delays 0-0, Black will complete his development with ... &e6, ... &d7, ... 0-0 or 0-0-0, and possibly ... a7-a6 (to provide a retreat for the valuable Bishop on c5 if White tries &a4). White may try f2-f4, though it weakens the a7-g1 diagonal.

After **4 &g2 &c6 5 &f3** (instead of 5 &ge2) 5 ... d6 6 d3, Black should take time out for 6 ... a6. Because White's Knight at f3 blocks

his f-pawn, he is not threatening to play f2-f4 right away and thus Black can afford one nondeveloping move. Usually Black will castle on the Kingside here, since ... h7-h5-h4 is less feasible with the Knight at f3. I don't see that White can make much progress in this position.

Now back to the main line, 3 &c4.

Position after 3 &c4

3 ...   &c6

Again, there are four choices: 3 ... &c6, 3 ... &c5, 3 ... &xe4!?, and 3 ... &b4.

3 ... &c5 shows Black's willingness to transpose into the Giuoco Piano with 4 &f3 &c6 (see Part 2, after 1 e4 e5 2 &f3 &c6 3 &c4 &c5 4 d3 d6 5 &c3 &f6). But instead, White can head for a King's Gambit Declined with 4 d3 d6 5 f4 &c6 6 &f3, producing a position that normally arises from 1 e4 e5 2 f4 &c5 3 &f3 d6 4 &c4 &c6 5 &c3 &f6 6 d3 (Part 8). 3 ... &c5 thus has little independent value; it usually transposes to another opening.

The variation that puzzled Weaver Adams starts with **3 ... ♘xe4!?.**

Position after 3 ... ♘xe4

Because neither **4 ♘xe4? d5** nor **4 ♗xf7+? ♚xf7 5 ♘xe4 d5** is satisfactory for White, analysts suggested **4 ♕h5!? ♘d6 5 ♗b3** (5 ♕xe5+ ♕e7 is only equal) **5 ... ♘c6,** when White has a forced win of a Rook: **6 ♘b5!** (threatening 7 ♘xd6+ followed by mate on f7) **6 ... g6 7 ♕f3** (renewing the threat) **7 ... f5 8 ♕d5!** (once more!) **8 ... ♕e7 9 ♘xc7+ ♚d8 10 ♘xa8 b6.** But White's Knight is doomed, and Black will get a ferocious attack, gaining time by harassing White's Queen. In practice, White's results were so bad that Adams, in disgust, abandoned 6 ♘b5!. But **11 d3 ♗b7 12 h4** (threatening 13 ♗g5) **12 ... f4 13 ♕f3! ♘d4 14 ♕g4** (threatening to trade Queens with 15 ♕g5) **14 ... ♗h6 15 ♘h3** and White has consolidated, as later researches showed. However, the point is

academic: Black can simply play **5 ... ♗e7!** (instead of 5 ... ♘c6). After 6 ♕xe5 0-0 or 6 ♘f3 ♘c6 7 ♘xe5 0-0, White has no advantage. At the present time, 3 ... ♘xe4!? is considered to equalize.

The other possibility, **3 ... ♗b4,** plans ... c7-c6 and ... d7-d5. White should react with 4 ♘f3 d6 5 0-0, when Black has nothing better than to transpose to the main line with 5 ... ♘c6 6 d3.

Finally, **3 ... ♘c6** is the most flexible move. Black develops his Knight to a very desirable square, defends e5 and d4, and doesn't commit his King Bishop prematurely.

4 d3

A modest decision, but the alternative **4 f4?** is virtually refuted by 4 ... ♘xe4! 5 ♘f3 (5 ♘xe4 d5 regains the piece favorably) **5 ... ♘d6!** (not 5 ... ♘xc3? 6 dxc3 exf4 7 ♗xf4, and White is way ahead in development) 6 ♗b3 e4!. If White wins back his pawn with 7 ♘g5 h6 8 ♘gxe4, then 8 ... ♘xe4 9 ♕e2 (9

♘xe4 ♕e7 10 ♕e2 ♘d4) 8 ...
♘d4! 9 ♕xe4+ ♕e7 gives Black
the sounder pawn structure (White's
advanced f-pawn weakens White's
position) and a slight advantage
overall.

Also bad is 4 ♘f3? ♘xe4!. This
"fork trick" is a recurrent motif in
the battle for the center. After 5
♘xe4 d5 6 ♗d3 dxe4 7 ♗xe4 ♗d6,
Black has the stronger center. Even
worse is 5 ♗xf7+? ♔xf7 6 ♘xe4
d5 7 ♘eg5+ ♔g8. Black's King
will reach safety by ... h7-h6 and ...
♔h7 and his King Rook will be
developed to f8 or e8 after the King
Bishop moves. White's Knight at g5
will be forced (by ... h7-h6) to
retreat to the poor square h3, and
White will be left with fewer pawns
in the center. Black has the much
better game.

4 ...   ♗b4

Black pins White's Knight, there-
by reducing White's grip on d5.
Less logical is 4 ... ♘a5?! because
White calmly ignores the threat!
After 5 ♘ge2! ♘xc4 6 dxc4 d6 7
0-0 ♗e6 8 b3, it's difficult for
Black to obtain active play because
White's pawns at c4 and e4 exert
pressure on d5, preventing ... d7-
d5. The half-open d-file also helps
White.

5 ♘f3!

One of Larsen's discoveries was
that Black's defense is none too
easy after this unpretentious move.
After 5 ♘e2?! Black can open

the center with 5 ... d5! 6 exd5
♘xd5. He will support his Knight
on d5 with ... ♗e6; exchanges simplify the position without changing
the verdict of equality.

One merit of 5 ♗g5 is that it
stops ... d7-d5. But 5 ... h6! "puts
the question" to the Bishop. If it
retreats, Black can break the pin at
any time with ... g7-g5. For
instance, 6 ♗h4 d6 7 ♘e2 ♗e6 8
0-0? allows 8 ... g5! 9 ♗g3 h5!,
when White will soon be buried
under an avalanche of pawns. If
White plays 6 ♗xf6, with the idea 6
... ♕xf6 7 ♘e2! followed by 0-0
and ♘d5, Black interpolates 6 ...
♗xc3+ ! 7 bxc3 before 7 ... ♕xf6,
and the route to d5 is blocked by
the White pawn on c3. Once again,
Black has equality.

5 ...   d6

Now 5 ... d5?! doesn't work so
well because of 6 exd5 ♘xd5 7
0-0!. Black can't comfortably
support his Knight with 7 ... ♗e6 8
♘g5! ♘xc3 (8 ... ♗xc3 9 ♘xe6!) 9
♘xe6! ♘xd1 10 ♘xd8 ♖xd8 11
♖xd1 because White gets the edge
in the endgame due to his powerful
unopposed King Bishop. But accepting White's sacrifice by 7 ...
♘xc3 8 bxc3 ♗xc3 allows 9 ♘g5!.
White threatens f7 and plots ♗a3
and ♕h5.

6 0-0

Breaking the pin. Now Black
should take the Knight before
White can play 7 ♗g5 and 8 ♘d5.

6 ...   ♗xc3

With this move and the next two, Black exchanges the two White minor pieces that observe d5. This eases his game and gives him near equality.

7 bxc3   ♘a5!
8 ♗b3

This time White can't ignore the threat of 8 ... ♘xc4 because his tripled pawns would be very vulnerable to attack by ... ♗e6 and ... ♘d7-b6.

8 ...   ♘xb3
9 axb3   0-0

White's strange pawn formation is the root of his tiny advantage. His pawns are closer to the center and help to control it. He can advance f2-f4, with the idea either of storming the Kingside with f4-f5-f6 (possibly aided by g2-g4-g5) or opening the f-file with fxe5. Although there are no perceptible

weaknesses in Black's position, he suffers from passivity. The only pawn push that would free his position is ... d6-d5, but White can immediately prohibit it.

Instructive Game

White: Bent Larsen
Black: L. Lengyel

Interzonal Tournament
Amsterdam 1964

1 e4	e5
2 ♗c4	♘f6
3 ♘c3	♘c6
4 d3	♗b4
5 ♘f3	d6
6 0-0	♗xc3
7 bxc3	♘a5
8 ♗b3	♘xb3
9 axb3	0-0
10 c4	♕e7

In a game played several rounds earlier in the same tournament, Gligoric tried 10 ... b6 11 ♕e2 ♘d7 12 ♗g5 f6 13 ♗e3 ♖e8 14 ♘d2 ♘f8 15 f4 exf4 16 ♗xf4. White's extra space may still give him an edge, but

Gligoric drew this game against Larsen.

11	♘d2	♘d7
12	♕h5	♘c5

Threatening 13 ... ♘e6, to prevent f2-f4.

13	f4!	exf4
14	♖xf4	♕e5
15	♕xe5	dxe5
16	♖f2	

There follows a long period of maneuvering. White wants to threaten g2-g4-g5, but Black defends well. Sooner or later, White must attempt to advance c2-c3 and d3-d4. In the meantime, he avoids giving Black a favorable opportunity for ... f7-f5.

16	...	♘e6
17	♘f3	f6
18	♗e3	a6
19	♘h4	♗d7
20	♘f5	♖ae8
21	h3	♖f7
22	♔h2	♘f8
23	g4	♘g6
24	♘g3	♘e7
25	♖af1	♗e6
26	♘e2	

26 g5 fxg5 is fine for Black.

26	...	♘c6
27	♔g3	♘b8
28	♘c3	c6

A concession, but 29 ♘d5 would have been very annoying.

29	c5!	

White aims at the new weaknesses on b6 and d6.

29	...	♘d7
30	♘a4	♖d8
31	h4	♖df8
32	♘b2	♖c8
33	♖a1	♔f8
34	♖a4!	♔e8
35	♖b4	♖c7
36	c3	g6?

Black handled the threat of ♘c4-d6 in stride (his answer would have been ... ♗xc4), but he panics at White's central action. A waiting strategy is necessary.

37	d4	h5

If Black had intended 37 ... f5, he now noticed that 38 gxf5 gxf5 39 exf5 ♗xf5 would have allowed 40 ♘c4!.

38	g5!	fxg5
39	♗xg5	exd4
40	♖xf7	♔xf7
41	cxd4	♘f6
42	♔f4	

White's next goal is d4-d5.

42	...	a5!?
43	♖a4	♗xb3
44	♖xa5	♘g4
45	♖a3	♗e6
46	♘d3	♔g7
47	♘e5	♖c8

Larsen is not concerned about the drawish reputation of the opposite-color Bishops, since his King continually threatens to penetrate into Black's position via the dark squares.

48	♗e7	♖e8
49	♗d6	♘xe5
50	♗xe5 +	♔f7
51	♔g5	♗g4
52	♖a1	♖e6
53	♖b1!	♖e7
54	♖f1 +	♔e8
55	♔xg6	

Winning the pawn doesn't give White a passed pawn, but now Black's h-pawn is under attack and White is getting ready to play d4-d5. Black's Bishop cannot handle both threats!

55	...	♔d7
56	♖f4	♗e2

57	♗d6	♖e6 +
58	♔g5	♗d3
59	♗e5!	

Of course, 59 e5? would allow Black to blockade on the light squares.

59	...	♗e2
60	♖f2	♗d3
61	♔f4	♖g6
62	♔e3	♗c4
63	♖f5	♖g1
64	♖xh5	♖e1 +
65	♔f4	♗d3
66	♖h7 +	♔e6?!

Hopeless is 66 ... ♔e8 67 ♖xb7 anyway.

67	d5 + !	cxd5
68	exd5 +	♔xd5
69	♖d7 +	**Black resigns**

If 69 ... ♔c4, then 70 ♖d4 + ♔c3 71 ♖e4 + ! ♔d2 72 ♗c3 + ! ♔xc3 73 ♖xe1 wins.

Part Ten
Other Openings

Jack Peters

Ponziani Opening

White	Black
1 e4	e5
2 ♘f3	♘c6
3 c3	

White's idea in the Ponziani Opening is to create a strong pawn center by playing d2-d4 and recapturing on d4 (if Black plays ... exd4) with another pawn. As in most 1 e4 openings, having pawns side by side on e4 and d4 is very desirable; they control many important squares in the center and give White more space than Black. But Black need not fear the Ponziani, for he can equalize easily. The Ponziani should be classed among the "harmless" openings.

Unfortunately for White, the move 3 c3 does not threaten anything besides 4 d4. Black can use the respite to counterattack, and White never seems to find time to establish dominance over the center.

3 ...	♘f6!

The choice of grandmasters, revealing another defect of 3 c3: White can't develop his Queen Knight to the normal square c3, so he has no handy defense for his pawn at e4. In addition, Black takes the lead in development.

The sharpest reply is **3 ... d5!?**.

Position after 3 ... d5

117

This move also has a fine reputation, but it entails more risk than the safe, effective 3 ... ♘f6!. White's usual response is to attack the e-pawn by pinning the Black Knight at c6 with 4 ♕a4 or 4 ♗b5. Black can answer either move with 4 ... f6, which looks strange because it takes f6 away from Black's King Knight, but the move strengthens Black's center by supporting the pawn at e5. After **4 ♕a4 f6 5 ♗b5** (or **4 ♗b5 f6**, when 5 ♕a4 is still best!), Black defends with 5 ... ♘e7 6 exd5 ♕xd5 7 d4 ♗d7 or 7 ... ♗g4. Black will parry White's eventual threat of c3-c4 and d4-d5 by playing ... exd4. At the moment, 8 c4? is a mistake because 8 ... ♕e4+! and 9 ... exd4 saves Black.

The complications arise when Black meets 4 ♕a4 with **4 ... ♗d7?!** 5 exd5 ♘d4 (or 5 ... ♘b4 6 ♕b3!, keeping the extra pawn) 6 ♕d1!, or with **4 ... ♘f6!?** 5 ♘xe5 ♗d6 6 ♘xc6 bxc6 7 d3! 0-0 8 ♗e2!. In neither variation does Black have enough compensation for the pawn, although White must play carefully to avoid falling behind in development. I think 4 ... ♘f6!? almost works, but 4 ... ♗d7?! seems inadequate.

After 3 ... d5 **4 ♗b5**, Black might do better with **4 ... dxe4!** than with 4 ... f6. His idea appears in the sequence 5 ♘xe5 ♕d5! 6 ♕a4 (cleverly protecting his Knight by the threat to capture on c6) 6 ... ♘e7, and now White's Knight at e5

is really threatened. White doesn't want to help Black develop with 7 ♘xc6 ♘xc6, but 7 f4 (threatening 8 ♗c4 and 9 ♘xf7) 7 ... ♗d7! 8 ♘xd7 (8 ♗c4?? loses a piece to 8 ... ♘xe5! 9 ♗xd5 ♘d3+! 10 ♔e2 ♗xa4) 8 ... ♔xd7! leaves White with a backward d-pawn which interferes with the normal development of his Queenside. Black will break the pin with ... a7-a6 and castle "by hand" with ... ♖d8 and ... ♔c8. The chances are roughly equal. If this analysis is correct, then 4 ♕a4 is preferable to 4 ♗b5.

Position after 3 ... ♘f6

4 d4

Defensive moves like 4 d3, 4 ♕c2, and 4 ♗d3 allow Black to strike in the center with 4 ... d5!.

4 ...   ♘xe4

Shattering White's dream center. The tempting alternative **4 ... d5!?**

is rebuffed by 5 ♗b5! exd4 (5 ...
♘xe5? 6 ♘xe5 ♗d7 looks
promising, but 7 ♕b3! finds the
Achilles Heel of Black's game—the
d-pawn: if 7 ... ♘f6 8 ♗g5 or 7 ...
♘xe5 8 ♕xd5!, Black loses a pawn)
6 e5 ♘e4 7 ♘xd4. Thus we reach a
position from the Two Knights
Defense (1 e4 e5 2 ♘f3 ♘c6 3 ♗c4
♘f6 4 d4 exd4 5 e5 d5 6 ♗b5 ♘e4
7 ♘xd4), with the difference that
White has the extra move c2-c3,
which must help. Compare Part
Three of this book.

5 d5

5 dxe5? is inadvisable. The
cautious 5 ... d5 and the bold 5 ...
♗c5! 6 ♕d5 ♗xf2+ 7 ♔d1 f5!
both favor Black.

5 ...   ♘e7

The most interesting try involves
a piece sacrifice: **5 ... ♗c5?!** 6 dxc6
♗xf2+ (6 ... ♘xf2? 7 ♕d5! ♘xh1
8 ♕xc5 should win for White, since
Black's Knight will be captured) 7
♔e2 bxc6 (threatening 8 ... ♗a6
mate!) 8 ♕a4! f5 9 ♘bd2!. Black
will end up with two center pawns
for the Knight, but White's King
will escape to c2. White should
have the better game.

Also playable, though rather
timid, is **5 ... ♘b8.** Then 6 ♘xe5
♗c5!? leads to obscure complications after 7 ♕g4! 0-0! 8 ♕xe4
d6. White can't keep the extra piece
because Black threatens to pin
White's Queen with 9 ... ♖e8. If

White doesn't care for obscure
complications, he can assure
himself of equality with **6 ♗d3**
♘c5 7 ♘xe5 ♘xd3+ 8 ♘xd3.
Black will be slower than White in
mobilizing his Queenside forces
because of the "undeveloping" 5 ...
♘b8, but White's slight edge in
development should soon
evaporate.

With 5 ... ♘e7 Black blocks his
King Bishop, but he will move the
Knight to g6.

6 ♘xe5

Else White stays a pawn down.

6 ...   ♘g6
7 ♗d3

Setting a trap: 7 ... ♘xf2?
(hoping for 8 ♔xf2? ♘xe5) loses to
8 ♗xg6! ♘xd1 (8 ... hxg6 9 ♕xf2
wins a piece) 9 ♗xf7+ ♔e7 10
♗g5+ ♔d6 11 ♘c4+! ♔c5 12
♘ba3! (threatening 13 b4 mate) 12
... a5 13 ♗xd8, and White emerges
two pieces ahead! However, Black
can get an even game by avoiding
this trap.

White's other choices at move
seven promise nothing better than
equality anyway.

7 ♕d4 ♕f6! 8 ♕xe4 (8 ♘xg6?
♕xd4 9 cxd4 hxg6 gives Black
chances to win White's pawn at d5
after ... ♘f6) 8 ... ♕xe5 trades
Queens, producing a lifeless position and an almost certain draw.

7 ♘xg6?! hxg6 is worse for
White. Black can use his Rook

actively on the h-file, especially if White risks castling on the Kingside.

7 ...   ♘xe5!

Eliminating White's central Knight seems stronger than 7 ... ♘c5 8 ♗xg6, though that is not dangerous for Black either.

8   ♗xe4   ♗c5

Black's chances are fully equal. Variations like these are responsible for the Ponziani Opening's "harmless" reputation.

Philidor Defense

White	Black
1 e4	e5
2 ♘f3	d6

The Philidor Defense has acquired a reputation as a dull, passive defense in which Black struggles to get a half-point from a horribly cramped game. While there is some truth in this view, it does not tell the whole story. Some variations, including the main line, do give Black a cramped position; but others lead to wild complications and wide-open attacking play. Only time will tell whether the Philidor will become a reliable defense of the future or a relic of the past.

2 ... d6 is a very tempting move. In the Ruy Lopez, White's idea is to exert lasting pressure on Black's pawn at e5. But by playing 2 ... d6 Black defends the e-pawn securely and the Ruy Lopez strategy loses its effectiveness. If White was hoping for some obscure variation of the Scotch, Giuoco Piano, Ponziani, or Four Knights Game, after 2 ... d6 he suddenly finds himself stuck in Black's choice of opening.

But before you imagine that the Philidor is the answer to your dreams when you play Black, you should realize that there are two serious drawbacks to it.

First, 2 ... d6 shuts in Black's King Bishop. Although e7 is often a suitable square for the Bishop, it's too early to forsake the option of playing the Bishop to a more active post on c5 or b4.

Second, 2 ... d6 is inferior to 2 ... ♘c6 in controlling d4. After 2 ... ♘c6 3 d4 exd4 4 ♘xd4 (see Part Five), note that Black's Knight is attacking White's. After 2 ... d6 3 d4 exd4 4 ♘xd4, White's Knight is not in danger and thus White has a freer hand in continuing his development.

Neither of these drawbacks is fatal, but they tend to give White a more durable edge against the Philidor than he obtains against 2 ... ♘c6. The Philidor is, among strong players, the most popular of the less common openings examined in this chapter, and, unlike the others, is occasionally ventured even by some grandmasters.

3   d4

White seizes space in the center, renews the threat to Black's e-pawn, and opens the c1-h6 diagonal for his Queen Bishop. One could hardly expect more from a move. Still, there is a worthy alternative in 3 ♗c4!?.

If Black had intended to answer 3 d4 with 3 ... ♘d7 or 3 ... f5, he can answer 3 ♗c4 in the same way. But, if he had planned 3 ... exd4 or 3 ... ♘f6, he must revise his strategy. After 3 ♗c4 he can't play 3 ... ♘f6? because of 4 ♘g5! d5 5 exd5 ♘xd5 6 ♕f3 (double attack) 6 ... ♕xg5 7 ♗xd5, attacking b7 and

f7. Now 7 ... ♕e7 8 ♗xb7 e4!? fails to 9 ♕b3! (9 ♗xe4? f5), so Black must cede at least a pawn by 7 ... ♕f6 or 7 ... ♕f4.

Not sufficient for Black is 3 ♗c4 ♗e6? because of 4 ♗xe6 fxe6 5 d4! (White must act at once) 5 ... exd4 6 ♘xd4. Black has problems defending e6; 6 ... ♕f6 7 ♕h5 + ! ♕f7 (7 ... g6 8 ♕b5 + ♘d7 9 ♕xb7 ♖b8 10 ♕xa7 successfully grabs two pawns) 8 ♕h3!, and 6 ... e5 7 ♘e6! ♕e7 8 ♕h5 + ! g6 9 ♕h3 are too awkward.

If Black is willing to play the Hungarian Defense (3 ... ♗e7 in Part Two), he can meet 3 ♗c4 with 3 ... ♘c6 4 d4 ♗e7. Otherwise, he should settle for 3 ... ♗e7 4 d4 exd4, which is covered below under 3 d4 exd4 4 ♘xd4.

For White, 3 ♗c4!? is a handy, no-risk method of decreasing Black's options at the third move. I'm surprised that White doesn't try it more often.

3   ...   ♘f6

Black counterattacks against White's pawn at e4. Modern opening theory says that 3 ... ♘f6 improves on the older 3 ... ♘d7 variation because it nearly forces White into the "ideal" position after seven moves that Black wants, whereas 3 ... ♘d7 lets White choose between that position and another promising alternative. If we examine 3 ... ♘d7 more closely, we'll see the difference.

After **3 ... ♘d7 4 ♗c4,** Black's only good move is **4 ... c6!**, the Hanham Variation. Inadequate are 4 ... ♘gf6? 5 dxe5! ♘xe5 (or 5 ... dxe5 6 ♘g5!) 6 ♘xe5 dxe5 7 ♗xf7+! ♔xf7 8 ♕xd8 ♗b4+ 9 ♕d2! ♗xd2+ 10 ♘bxd2, winning a pawn for White, and 4 ... ♗e7? 5 dxe5! ♘xe5 (5 ... dxe5? 6 ♕d5! is even worse) 6 ♘xe5 dxe5 7 ♕h5!, again winning a pawn. But 4 ... c6! handles 5 ♘g5 with 5 ... ♘h6!.

So, "best play" after 3 ... ♗d7 4 ♗c4 c6! is **5 ♘c3 ♗e7.** White may transpose to the main line with 6 0-0 ♘gf6 7 a4 0-0, but the startling **6 dxe5 dxe5 7 ♘g5!** is more enterprising.

After 3 ... ♘d7 4 ♗c4 c6 5 ♘c3 ♗e7 6 dxe5 dxe5 7 ♘g5

White's point is 7 ... ♗xg5 8 ♕h5!, regaining the piece because of the mate threat. Neither 8 ... g6 9 ♕xg5 nor 8 ... ♕f6 9 ♗xg5 ♕g6 10 ♕h4! equalizes. White's active pieces, particularly his Bishops, outshine Black's poorly developed forces.

If Black meets 7 ♘g5! with 7 ... ♘h6, White's Knight stuns him again with 8 ♘e6!. The variations are complex, but 8 ... fxe6 9 ♗xh6 ♘b6! (9 ... gxh6 10 ♕h5+ ♔f8 11 ♗xe6 ♕e8 12 ♕xh6 is mate!) 10 ♕h5+ ♔f8 11 ♗b3 gxh6 12 ♖d1 makes White's attack too powerful. The "Rook lift" ♖d3-f3 adds more ammunition.

Because 6 dxe5 dxe5 7 ♘g5! leaves Black in difficulties, Black usually steers for the main line by way of 3 ... ♘f6 rather than 3 ... ♘d7.

Besides 3 ... ♘d7, Black has two radically different paths at move three: 3 ... f5? and 3 ... exd4.

Philidor himself is supposed to have recommended 2 ... d6 so that Black could play 3 ... f5, and Paul Morphy liked 3 ... f5 against both 3 ♗c4 and 3 d4. Yet **3 ... f5** is absolutely unsound! Each of the four logical replies (4 ♗c4, 4 ♘c3, 4 dxe5, and 4 exf5) clearly favors White! We will look at the two most convincing.

Position after 3 ... f5

4 ♗c4! exploits the weakened a2-g8 diagonal leading to the area of Black's King and threatens 5 ♘g5 and 5 dxe5. After 4 ... fxe4 5 ♘xe5! Black can't take the Knight because 5 ... dxe5 6 ♕h5+ ♔d7 7 ♕f5+! ♔c6 8 ♕xe5 pushes his King into a comical position. But 5 ... d5 6 ♕h5+ g6 7 ♘xg6! ♘f6! doesn't save him either, since 8 ♕e5+ ♗e7 9 ♗b5+! (simpler than 9 ♘xh8 dxc4) 9 ... c6 10 ♘xe7! ♕xe7 11 ♕xe7+ ♔xe7 12 ♗e2 keeps an extra pawn.

Also forcing is **4 dxe5!** fxe4 5 ♘g5 d5 6 e6!, threatening 7 ♘f7. Then 6 ... ♘h6 7 ♘c3 c6 8 ♘gxe4! (otherwise Black escapes) 8 ... fxe4 (8 ... ♗xe6! 9 ♕h5+ ♔d7 is a little better) 9 ♕h5+ g6 10 ♕e5 ♖g8 11 ♗g5! should win. Notice the pretty checkmate after 11 ... ♕d6? 12 ♖d1! ♕xe6 (12 ... ♕xe5 13 ♖d8 mate) 13 ♗c4!.

With **3 ... exd4**, Black avoids such direct threats. He intends to develop economically, if not aggressively, with ... ♘f6, ... ♗e7

Position after 3 ... exd4

or ... ♗g7, ... 0-0, and ... ♘c6. But White can use his space advantage to place his pieces on very desirable squares.

Probably best is **4 ♕xd4!**. Despite the principle that the Queen should not be brought out too early in the game, White is ready with an answer to Black's natural attempt to exploit the "mistake": 4 ... ♘c6 5 ♗b5! ♗d7 6 ♗xc6 ♗xc6, and the Queen is secure on d4. Continuing 7 ♗g5! ♘f6 8 ♘c3 ♗e7 9 0-0-0 0-0 10 ♖he1, White quickly completes his development and plans to break open the center with e4-e5 before Black mobilizes the rest of his pieces.

Players who don't like to exchange a Bishop for a Knight unnecessarily may prefer **4 ♘xd4** to 4 ♕xd4. Certainly 4 ♘xd4 ♘f6 5 ♘c3 ♗e7 6 ♗f4! (planning 0-0-0) 6 ... 0-0 7 ♕d2 ♘c6 8 0-0-0 gives White excellent attacking chances on the Kingside with little risk. He might advance g2-g4, h2-h4, g4-g5, and h4-h5, storming Black's Kingside with pawns. After driving away Black's King Knight, he could expose Black's King with g5-g6 or h5-h6.

But recently this variation of the Philidor (3 ... exd4 4 ♘xd4) has been revitalized for Black with the idea **4 ...g6!**. His King Bishop will exert more pressure on White's center from g7 than from e7, and with no Bishop on e7, his Rook will have more scope on e8. After 4 ... g6 5 ♘c3 ♗g7 6 ♗f4 ♘f6 7 ♕d2 0-0 8 0-0-0 ♖e8, for instance, White must take time out for 9 f3. Black is almost equal after 9 ... ♘c6! (or 9 ... ♘bd7), and 9 ... a6!?, intending ... b7-b5, envisions a pawn storm of his own.

Let's return to the main line, 3 ... ♘f6.

Position after 3 ... ♘f6

4 ♘c3

This is the most common move, although White can obtain a slight advantage by 4 dxe5 ♘xe4 5 ♕d5! (5 ♗c4 c6! is fine for Black) 5 ... ♘c5 6 ♗g5! ♗e7 7 exd6 ♕xd6 8 ♘c3!, thanks to his rapid development. In contrast to most positions in the Philidor Defense, the center pawns have all been exchanged, leaving two open files.

4 ... ♘bd7

Black still has the option of 4 ... exd4, as on move three.

5 ♗c4

A good developing move that threatens 6 ♘g5.

5 ... ♗e7

Black develops his Bishop to the only available square, and prepares to castle.

Position after 5 ... ♗e7

6 0-0

White has two tactical tries that don't quite succeed. If **6 ♘g5?!** 0-0 7 ♗xf7+ ♖xf7 8 ♘e6! (the point; 8 ♘xf7? ♔xf7 favors Black because in the middlegame the two pieces will be more valuable than the Rook and pawn) 8 ... ♕e8 9 ♘xc7 ♕d8 10 ♘xa8 gains material, but then comes 10 ... b5! threatening both 11 ... ♗b7, winning the trapped Knight, and 11 ... b4, winning the e-pawn. If 11 ♘xb5, then 11 ... ♕a5+ 12 ♘c3 ♘xe4! 13 0-0 ♘xc3 14 bxc3 ♗b7 wins the Knight. The activity of

Black's pieces guarantees him attacking chances, and this compensates for his material deficit. Inserting 6 dxe5 dxe5 changes a detail or two of this line of play, but not its overall evaluation.

The second attempt is **6 ♗xf7 + ?** ♔xf7 7 ♘g5 + ♔g8 (best) 8 ♘e6 ♕e8 9 ♘xc7 ♕g6! (this time Black's counterattack comes on the Kingside!) 10 ♘xa8 ♕xg2 11 ♖f1 exd4! 12 ♕xd4 ♘e5!. Although he is behind in material, Black has a winning attack, with threats of ... ♘f3 + and ... ♗h3.

Because 11 ... exd4 was a useful move in this last variation, now it makes sense for White to prevent it by prefacing ♗xf7 + with **6 dxe5.** This does indeed pose more problems. After 6 ... dxe5 7 ♗xf7 + !? ♔xf7 8 ♘g5 + ♔g8 9 ♘e6 ♕e8 10 ♘xc7 ♕g6 11 ♘xa8 ♕xg2 12 ♖f1, Black can't play 12 ... ♘e5, as in the other line. He has nothing better than 12 ... ♘c5 13 ♕e2 ♗h3!, which recovers the Exchange and results in approximately equal chances. If this isn't enough, Black can risk 8 ... ♔g6!? 9 f4! (9 ♘e6? ♕g8! 10 ♘xc7 ♖b8 holds) 9 ... exf4 10 ♘e6 ♕g8! 11 ♘xc7 ♖b8 12 ♗xf4. White's two extra pawns are almost equivalent to the Bishop, and he has many opportunities to attack Black's misplaced King. It's a shame this interesting position isn't tested in master play.

6 ...   0-0

7 a4

White realizes that Black will play 7 ... c6, and he anticipates the threat of ... b7-b5. Also quite playable is 7 ♕e2 c6 8 a4.

7 ...   c6

This is the critical position of the main line of the Philidor Defense.

This position sometimes arises from 3 ... ♘d7 4 ♗c4 c6! 5 ♘c3 ♗e7 6 0-0 ♘gf6 7 a4 0-0, but that move order allows White to deviate profitably with 6 dxe5 dxe5 7 ♘g5!, as discussed earlier.

White has more space and some chances to attack on the Kingside, usually by ♘h4-f5. But there are no weaknesses in Black's camp. White should therefore strive to maintain his spatial advantage while maneuvering his pieces to provoke Black into creating weaknesses. He should try to avoid playing dxe5, since the reply ... dxe5 relieves

Black's cramp by giving him the use of c5 and b4. Exchanging pawns in the center is good for White only if it allows him to invade along the d-file.

Black's strategy is easy to describe but difficult to execute. First, he wants to complete his development with ... ♛c7, ... b7-b6, and ... ♝b7. Then he wants to advance on the Queenside with ... a7-a6 and ... b6-b5. This gains more room to maneuver (b6 for the Knight) and threatens to advance farther with ...b5-b4. He has no active play on the Kingside, so his goal there is just to stymie White's attack. If White exchanges in the center with dxe5, Black must be ready to recapture with the d-pawn. If he has to recapture with a piece, then White can make use of the squares d4 and f4 while the pawn at d6 remains backward and weak. Black should try to provoke dxe5 by making threats of ... d6-d5 or ... exd4, although these threats will not necessarily be carried out. A standard way to reshuffle his pieces is ... ♜e8, ... ♞f8-e6, and ... ♝f8. If White does exchange on e5, Black may be able to dispense with ... b7-b6 and develop his Bishop on e6, where it opposes White's King Bishop.

It takes a patient player to handle Black's position. Here's an example of how to do it.

Instructive Game No. 1

White: L. Stein
Black: T. Petrosian

Moscow 1971

1	e4	e5
2	♞f3	d6
3	d4	♞f6
4	♞c3	♞bd7
5	♝c4	♝e7
6	0-0	0-0
7	a4	c6
8	a5!?	

White will open the a-file if Black advances ... b7-b6.

8	...	h6

Preventing ♞g5 so he can play ... ♜e8 without having to worry about his f-pawn. If 8 ... b6? or 8 ... b5?, White replies 9 axb6 ♞xb6 10 ♝a6!, and Black's pawns at a7, c6, and e5 are vulnerable.

9	♝a2	

More natural is 9 ♜e1 or 9 ♛e2

and 10 ♖d1, bearing down on the central files.

| 9 | ... | ♖e8 |
| 10 | dxe5?! | dxe5! |

Not 10 ... ♘xe5? because 11 ♘d4! threatens to chase Black back with f2-f4.

11	♕e2	♗f8
12	♖d1	♕c7
13	♘h4!	

White still has a tiny advantage, but Petrosian finds a way to safeguard his Kingside. Notice that 13 ... b6? 14 axb6 axb6? loses to 15 ♗xf7 + ! ♔xf7 16 ♖xa8.

| 13 | ... | ♘c5 |
| 14 | ♘f5 | ♔h7! |

A mistake is 14 ... ♗xf5? 15 exf5, for then White would launch a pawn storm with g2-g4, h2-h4, and g4-g5. Also, Black would lose the useful maneuvering square e6. And 14 ... ♘fxe4? (hoping for 15 ♘xe4? ♗xf5)

15 ♘xh6 + ! gxh6 16 ♘xe4 exposes Black's King.

| 15 | ♕f3 | |

Threatening 16 ♘xh6! gxh6 17 ♕xf6.

15	...	♘g8!
16	b4	♘e6
17	♖b1?!	

Better is 17 b5!, hoping to gain control of d5 by a5-a6xb7 and b5xc6.

17	...	g6
18	♘e3	♗g7
19	♘c4	♘d4!

Now Black has somewhat the better of it.

| 20 | ♕d3 | ♖d8 |
| 21 | ♕f1 | ♗e6?! |

Black can take the c-pawn, but because of his standing in the tournament Petrosian is content to draw.

| 22 | ♘e3 | **Draw** |

Black would have good reason to play on. Stein was lucky that Petrosian was not feeling more ambitious!

And here's an example of how things can go wrong in the Philidor.

Instructive Game No. 2

White: V. Tseshkovsky
Black: A. Lutikov

Alma-Ata, U.S.S.R., 1969

1	e4	e5
2	♘f3	d6
3	d4	♘f6
4	♘c3	♘bd7
5	♗c4	♗e7
6	0-0	0-0
7	a4	c6
8	♕e2	exd4?
9	♘xd4	♘xe4?!

Black starts a combination (the "fork trick") to destroy White's center, but the combination has a flaw in it. A move earlier he should have continued 8 ... b6 or 8 ... ♕c7.

10 ♘xe4!

White refrains from 10 ♕xe4 d5 11 ♗xd5 (11 ♘xd5? cxd5 12 ♗xd5 ♘f6 or 12 ♕xd5 ♘b6! 13 ♕xd8 ♖xd8 costs a piece) 11 ... ♘f6 12 ♗xf7+ ♖xf7, when Black's threats are more valuable than the pawn.

10	...	d5
11	♘f5!	dxc4?

This loses. Necessary is 11 ... dxe4 12 ♖d1! ♗f6 13 ♕xe4 ♕a5, though White keeps the advantage due to his control of the d-file and his well-placed Knight.

12 ♗h6! ♘f6

If 12 ... gxh6 13 ♕g4+ ♗g5 (forced) 14 ♘xh6+ ♔g7 15 ♘f5+ ♔g6 (15 ... ♔h8 16 ♘xg5) 16 f4! regains the piece.

13	♘eg3	♗xf5
14	♘xf5	gxh6
15	♘xe7+	♔g7
16	♘f5+	♔g6
17	♘e7+	♔g7
18	♕e5!	

The winning idea. White threatens 19 ♖ad1 and 20 ♖d6.

18 ... ♕b8

Or 18 ... ♖e8 19 ♖fe1.

19	♘f5+		♔g6
20	♘d6!		

Threatening 21 ♕g3+.

20	...		♔g7
21	♖fe1		♖d8
22	♖ad1		♖d7
23	♖d4!		♕c7

If 23 ... h5, then 24 ♕g5+ wins the Knight.

24	♖g4+	**Black resigns**

After 24 ... ♔f8 25 ♕xf6, Black gets mated on h8. This game proves the maxim, "a cramped game must be opened slowly."

Latvian Gambit

White	Black
1 e4	e5
2 ♘f3	f5

This move introduces the Latvian Gambit. Sometimes it is called the Greco Countergambit, after Giacchino Greco, one of the best players of the 17th century. But in the early 1900's a group of Latvian analysts devoted a lot of time to this defense, discovering much that is still the basis of what we know about this opening today, and they usually receive credit for the name.

Unlike 2 ... ♘c6 and 2 ... d6, the move 2 ... f5 doesn't defend Black's attacked e-pawn. Instead, Black counterattacks White's pawn at e4. In this respect, the Latvian Gambit is similar to the Petroff Defense (Part Six). However, Black's second move in the Petroff (2 ... ♘f6) is a very desirable developing move whereas 2 ... f5 develops nothing and exposes Black's King on the e8-h5 diagonal. One would therefore expect that the Latvian Gambit is inferior to the Petroff Defense, and analysis confirms that evaluation.

In spirit, the Latvian Gambit is more akin to the King's Gambit. But Black's attempt to play a King's Gambit with colors reversed must be viewed with suspicion, since the many solid defenses to the King's Gambit are even stronger with an extra move. Nevertheless, the opening is full of traps to catch the unwary.

3 ♘xe5

This simple reply produces the type of quiet position, favorable for White, that Black hoped to avoid

129

Position after 3 ♘xe5

with 2 ... f5. But if White wants a sharp battle from the start, he has two other promising choices.

The wildest is **3 ♗c4!?**. After **3 ... fxe4** (3 ... d6 is similar to the 3 ... f5 line in the Philidor), White answers **4 ♘xe5**, threatening 5 ♘f7. If 4 ... d5, White attacks with 5 ♕h5+ g6 6 ♘xg6!, so Black's usual response is **4 ... ♕g5**. Then **5 d4! ♕xg2 6 ♕h5+ g6 7 ♗f7+ ♔d8 8 ♗xg6!** offers a Rook.

Recent analysis suggests that Black's best chance is 8 ... ♕xh1+ 9 ♔e2 c6!, giving his King an outlet on c7. But 10 ♘c3 (threatening to win the Queen with 11 ♗g5+) 10 ... ♘f6 11 ♕h4 continues White's attack. Despite his extra Rook, Black's defense is extremely difficult.

Also complicated is **3 exf5** e4 (3 ... d6 4 d4 e4 5 ♘g5 ♗xf5 6 f3! opens the center favorably for White) 4 ♘e5! (threatening 5 ♕h5+) 4 ... ♘f6 5 ♗e2 d6 6 ♗h5+ ♔e7 (6 ... g6? 7 fxg6 dxe5? 8 g7+! makes a new Queen) 7 ♘f7 ♕e8 8 ♘xh8.

Although Black wins White's Bishop at h5 and traps White's Knight at h8, White's remaining pieces will come into play quickly, and Black may not actually get to capture the adventurous Knight.

3 ... ♕f6

Black has little choice, since White threatened both 4 ♕h5+ and 4 exf5.

4 ♘c4!

A fine alternative is 4 d4, when 4 ... d6 (4 ... fxe4? allows 5 ♗c4 and 6 ♘f7) 5 ♘c4 fxe4 6 ♘c3 develops rapidly. But White has other plans for his d-pawn!

4 ... fxe4
5 ♘c3 ♕g6

Protecting the e-pawn and freeing f6 for the Knight. Black can discourage d2-d3 with 5 ... ♕e6, but 6 ♘e3 threatens it again.

6 d3!

Here is White's idea. By eliminating the e-pawn, he removes Black's last foothold in the center. Because of his faster development, White's pieces will overrun Black's position.

Instructive Game

White: V. Smyslov
Black: M. Kamyshev

Moscow 1944

1	e4	e5
2	♘f3	f5
3	♘xe5	♛f6
4	♘c4	fxe4
5	♘c3	♛g6
6	d3	♗b4

Unfortunately for Black, he can't play 6 ... exd3 7 ♗xd3 (more development!) ♛xg2?? because of 8 ♛h5+! g6 9 ♛e5+ and 10 ♗e4, or if 8 ... ♔d8 9 ♗e4 ♘f6 10 ♗g5, winning material in either case.

7   ♗d2

This simple move develops another minor piece, breaks the pin, and renews the threat of 8 ♘xe4.

7	...	♗xc3
8	♗xc3	d5

No better is 8 ... ♘f6 9 ♗xf6! gxf6 10 dxe4 ♛xe4+ 11 ♘e3, when White will gain more time with 12 ♗d3. Black's split pawns on the Kingside don't shelter his King properly, either.

9	♘e5	♛f5
10	dxe4	♛xe4+

Or 10 ... dxe4 11 ♗c4!.

11	♗e2	♘f6
12	0-0	c6
13	♗h5+!	

Black has managed to anticipate White's threat to win his d-pawn with 13 ♗f3, but now White reveals another, more deadly threat.

13   ...   ♔f8

Neither 13 ... g6 14 ♖e1! nor 13 ... ♘xh5 14 ♛xh5+ g6 15 ♘xg6! saves Black.

14	♖e1	♛h4
15	♗g6!	

Much stronger than 15 ♗f3. The Bishop is safe on g6 because 15 ... hxg6 is met by 16 ♘xg6+, winning the Queen. Now the threat is 16 g3 (to drive the Queen away from protecting the b4-square) 16 ... ♕h3 17 ♗b4 + ♔g8 18 ♗f7 mate!

15 ...   ♘a6

Preventing ♗b4 + .

16 ♕e2!

Now the threat is 17 ♘f3 and 18 ♕e8 + !.

16 ...   ♗h3
17 ♘f3!   Black resigns

A Queen move permits 18 ♕e7 + ♔g8 19 ♕f7 mate.

Bishop Opening

White	Black
1 e4	e5
2 ♗c4	

The Bishop Opening has little independent character. The positions that arise from it may resemble those of the Vienna Game (Part Nine), the Giuoco Piano with 4 d3 (Part Two), and some other openings. Of the modern grandmasters, only Bent Larsen occasionally employs the Bishop Opening.

There was a time when 2 ♗c4 really worried Black. White immediately posts his Bishop on an excellent diagonal, eyes the vulnerable f7-square, and keeps open the option of f2-f4. But 2 ♗c4 does not contain a direct threat, and Black can use the breathing space to attack White's e-pawn with 2 ... ♘f6!. Today's rigorous opening analysis and excellent defensive technique have rendered the Bishop Opening harmless. Masters use it mainly for surprise value.

2 ...   ♘f6!

Almost an automatic response. In the nineteenth century Black often tried 2 ... ♗c5, which is sufficient for equality. After 2 ... ♗c5 Black answers 3 f4 with 3 ... ♗xg1! 4 ♕h5

(4 ♖xg1? ♕h4+ 5 g3 ♕xh2) 4 ...
♕e7 5 ♖xg1 ♘c6 followed by ...
♘f6. If 3 ♘f3 Black replies 3 ... ♘c6
(Part Two), and if 3 ♕e2!? ♘c6! 4
♗xf7+ ♔xf7 5 ♕c4+ d5! (the
reason Black ignored White's threat)
6 ♕xc5 dxe4. In the last variation,
Black's quicker development will
give him the advantage if White
snatches a pawn with 7 ♕c4+ ♗e6
8 ♕xe4 ♘f6. The realization that
Black can counterattack, at the
expense of a pawn, doomed the
Bishop Opening.

3 d3

For 3 ♘c3 see Part Nine, and for 3
♘f3 see Part Six.

With the modest 3 d3, White
abandons the usual open-games
strategy of preparing d2-d4 and
concentrates instead on f2-f4.
However, the lack of a threat enables
Black to seize the initiative in the
center, and White usually fails to
achieve even f2-f4.

More aggressive but unsound is **3
d4?!**. Black should accept the gambit
with 3 ... exd4 4 ♘f3 (4 ♕xd4 ♘c6
and 4 e5 d5! are strong for Black) 4
... ♘xe4! 5 ♕xd4 ♘f6, when White
doesn't have enough compensation
for the pawn. If 6 ♗g5 ♗e7 7 ♘c3,
then 7 ... c6! 8 0-0-0 d5 sets up a solid
formation. If this is not to Black's
taste, he can back out with 4 ... ♘c6,
which transposes to the 4 d4
variation of the Two Knights
Defense (Part Three).

| 3 | ... | c6 |

Black exploits White's timidity by
boldly planning to take over the
center with 4 ... d5. But a little too
bold is 3 ... d5? 4 exd5 ♘xd5 5 ♘f3
♘c6 6 0-0 ♗e7 7 ♖e1, and White's
central pressure is very annoying.
Neither 7 ... f6 8 d4! nor 7 ... ♗g4 8
h3 solves Black's problems.

4 ♘f3!

Admitting the failure of his f2-f4
plan. At the moment, 4 f4? exf4 5
♗xf4 d5! 6 exd5 ♘xd5! would
expose White's King more than
Black's.

But 4 ♘f3! reveals a sensible,
realistic evaluation of the position.
White discards his unworkable plan
and tries to point out the flaws in
Black's idea of ... d7-d5. He foresees
that Black's pawns at d5 and e5 will
be vulnerable, and he intends to put
pressure on them with moves like
♘c3, ♗g5, and (after 0-0) ♖e1.

Another clever try is **4 ♕e2!?**,
hoping to dissuade Black from ... d7-

133

d5 due to the threat to his e-pawn. But Black should go ahead with 4 ... d5! since 5 exd5 cxd5 6 ♛xe5+ ♝e7 develops quickly. It's probably too risky for White to grab the pawn. Black will gain more time by attacking the Queen with ... ♞c6 or (after ... 0-0) ... ♜e8.

| 4 | ... | d5 |
| 5 | ♝b3 | |

White can't win a pawn with 5 exd5? cxd5 6 ♝b5+ because of 6 ... ♝d7! 7 ♝xd7+ ♞bxd7, defending the pawn at e5.

| 5 | ... | ♝d6 |

Far from clear is 5 ... dxe4 6 ♞g5! (not 6 ♞xe5? ♛a5+!, forking King and Knight) 6 ... ♝e6, but 7 ♝xe6 fxe6 8 ♞xe4 is at least equal.

The text move fortifies Black's pawn center. A game Stahlberg-Weenink, 1930, continued 6 ♞c3 ♝e6 7 ♝g5 ♛a5 8 0-0 ♞bd7 9 ♜e1 0-0-0, with about even chances. Each player is carrying out his strategy: Black is occupying the center and gaining space while White is forcing Black to defend the pawns at d5 and e5.

Danish Gambit

White		Black
1	e4	e5
2	d4	exd4
3	c3	

Less logical is **3 ♛xd4,** the Center Game. After the natural response 3 ... ♞c6, White must move his Queen again, and there's no comfortable square. On a4 the Queen may be embarrassed by an eventual ... ♝d7. On d1 the Queen is safe, but Black gets a fine game after 4 ♛d1 ♞f6 5 ♞c3 ♝b4 6 ♝d2 d5!. The most popular choice, **4 ♛e3,** blocks White's Queen Bishop. Often the Queen will later step aside to g3, freeing the Bishop, but so many Queen moves in the opening can lead to trouble. White will trail in development; if the center is opened, Black's pieces will benefit.

The best answer to 4 ♕e3 is **4 ... ♘f6 5 ♘c3 ♗b4!** 6 ♗d2 0-0 7 0-0-0 ♖e8!. Already Black threatens ... d7-d5. The only sideline that Black needs to know is 5 e5 (instead of 5 ♘c3) 5 ... ♘g4 6 ♕e4. Then 6 ... d5! (not 6 ... ♘gxe5? 7 f4) 7 exd6 + ♗e6 gives Black a huge lead in development. He can meet 8 dxc7 with 8 ... ♕xc7 or 8 ... ♕d1 +! 9 ♔xd1 ♘xf2 + 10 ♔e1 ♘xe4.

With 3 c3 White aims for speedy development. He's willling to sacrifice one or two pawns to get the kind of position he wants—direct attack.

3   ...   dxc3

Black accepts the challenge. However, he can decline the gambit with **3 ... d5,** as in the Göring Gambit. In fact, 3 ... d5 4 exd5 ♕xd5 5 cxd4 ♘c6 6 ♘f3 transposes to a safe variation of the Göring. Black gets equality by 6 ... ♗g4 7 ♘c3 ♗b4!

4   ♗c4!

The start of the Danish Gambit proper, one of the most successful of the aggressive openings. White can still back out with **4 ♘xc3,** when 4 ... ♘c6 5 ♘f3 leads to the Göring Gambit (Part Five).

4   ...   cxb2
5   ♗xb2

Every amateur should experiment with this fascinating opening! There's no better way to learn the value of active pieces and fast development. Only when one fully understands these elements of attack can one accurately assess "wild" gambit positions. Even in "quiet" openings, there are surprising pawn sacrifices that transform the game into gambit-style play, so all players need the foundation of experience which the Danish Gambit, the Scotch and Göring Gambits, the King's Gambit, and other attacking openings provide.

It took years for the best players of the past to discover the correct defense to the Danish Gambit. White's Bishops, poised for attack, and his threat of ♕b3 immediately confront Black with serious problems.

5   ...   d5!

Returning a pawn blunts White's attack and catches up a bit in development. Much worse is 5 ...

♗b4 + ? ♔f1! ♘f6 7 e5 or 5 ... ♘f6?
6 e5! d5! (what else?) 7 exf6 dxc4 8
♕xd8 + ♔xd8 9 fxg7 ♗b4 + 10 ♘c3
♖g8 11 0-0-0 + , and White's advanced passed pawn and threat of
♘d5 will win.

6   ♗xd5

If 6 exd5, then 6 ... ♘f6 7 ♘c3
♗d6! prepares castling, and Black
survives. In time, his extra pawn
should bring him victory.

6   ...   ♗b4 + !

The move that killed the Danish!
For a while, the "refutation" was 6
... ♘f6 7 ♗xf7 + ! ♔xf7 8 ♕xd8
♗b4 + ! 9 ♕d2 (otherwise White
comes out a piece behind) 9 ...
♗xd2 + 10 ♘xd2 c5, when Black's
passed c-pawn supposedly gave him
the advantage. But 11 f4! activates
White's Kingside pawn majority,
and the game is still far from clear.

7   ♘c3

If 7 ♔f1, which threatens 8 ♗xg7
and 8 ♗xf7 + , Black must find the
beautiful defense 7 ... ♘f6! 8 ♕a4 +
♘c6! 9 ♗xc6 + bxc6 10 ♕xb4
♖b8!!. Because 11 ♕xb8? ♕d1
mate and 11 ♕c3 ♖xb2! 12 ♕xb2?
♕d1 mate both lose, White must
return the piece and remain a pawn
down.

7   ...   ♗xc3 +
8   ♗xc3   ♘f6!

Black will exchange his King
Knight for White's King Bishop and
emerge with an extra pawn, for
which White has little compensation.

Index of Complete Games

Index of Moves

INDEX OF MOVES

A
GUIDE
TO THE
CHESS OPENINGS

Do you know the difference between the Pirc Defense and the Modern Defense? Between the Grunfeld and the English? Do you know the precise move order of the Austrian Attack, the Benko Gambit, the several Samisch Variations?

The editors of R.H.M. have prepared a special booklet, "A Guide to the Chess Openings," to answer all these questions and dozens more. All major openings and variations are covered, move by move, with the correct name and move order in each case. Where applicable, transpositions are noted.

This valuable booklet is absolutely free! We offer it to you as a way of showing our appreciation for your interest in R.H.M. chess publications.

To get your free copy, just send your name and address as follows:

U.S., Canada, Mexico, Puerto Rico:	Europe and elsewhere:
GUIDE	**GUIDE**
R.H M. Press	R.H.M. Europe
172 Forest Avenue	110 Strand
Glen Cove, New York 11542	London WC2R OAA England

THE R.H.M. SURVEY OF CURRENT CHESS OPENINGS

LATEST GAMES ... LATEST THEORY

Our Survey devotes a *complete issue,* typically about 120 to 160 pages, to *one* opening, rather than dozens of openings. Previously, if a chess player wanted to study recent games in an opening in which he had a special interest, he had to pay for dozens of openings in which he had *no* interest. Not with the R.H.M. Survey!

For example, we have published our issue of the King's Indian Defence I, covering the Samisch, Four Pawns Attack, and Averbakh Variations, written by Petrosian, Szabo, Uhlmann, and Hartston, and containing more than 100 complete recent games. The *entire issue,* games and theory, concern only these variations of the King's Indian Defence. We have also published a complete Survey issue on the Kan Variation of the Sicilian Defence, with a brilliant 44-page essay by World Champion Anatoly Karpov and an analysis of latest theory by William Hartston, and this edition also includes a wide range of latest games. Our Survey on the Nimzo-Indian Defence, which includes *all* variations, was written by Ivkov, Keene, and Kaplan, and it too includes the latest games and latest theory on this important opening. Since this announcement was written, we have published other complete Surveys on other important openings.

Our Survey "team" is the finest! Lubosh Kavalek, current U.S. Champion, is Editor-in-Chief; Kevin O'Connell and Burt Hochberg are, respectively, Managing Editor and Executive Editor, and our Board of Contributing Editors includes 8 of the 10 top-rated chess grandmasters in the world, including 4 of the last 5 World Champions—Spassky, Petrosian, Botvinnik, and Tal—and the current World Champion, Anatoly Karpov. Little wonder, then, that our Surveys have already been highly praised for being authoritative, current, and complete!

All lines are presented with utmost clarity and are fully indexed so that you can turn immediately to the games and theory covering *exactly* what you want to study. Current analysis is written by top players, and the number of games in each line far exceeds anything available elsewhere.

We have no doubt that when you use our Surveys and realize that it keeps you completely up-to-date, tells you what's new and better for White or for Black in your favorite openings, you will become a devoted Survey subscriber. We do not have the space here to give you a full description of everything in our Surveys to help and guide your play. To receive full information in a very instructive descriptive folder, including sample Survey pages—there is no charge, no obligation—just send your name and address as follows:

U.S., Canada, Mexico, Puerto Rico:

CHESS SURVEY

R.H.M. Press
172 Forest Avenue
Glen Cove, New York 11542

Europe and elsewhere:

CHESS SURVEY

R.H.M. Europe
110 Strand
London WC2R OAA England

FREE

Important Booklet of Recent Open Games

We at R.H.M. Press appreciate the support you are giving our efforts to publish the finest in chess literature.

To show our appreciation, we want to send you a free booklet, containing a collection of important and instructive recent games in these openings, which we prepared after this book was printed.

To receive your copy—there is no charge or obligation—just send your name and address as follows:

U.S., Canada, Mexico, Puerto Rico:
OPEN GAMES

R.H.M. Press
172 Forest Avenue
Glen Cove, New York 11542

Europe and elsewhere:
OPEN GAMES

R.H.M. Europe
110 Strand
London WC2R OAA

NOTES

NOTES